To my wife Jeanne, living proof that
angels exist.

Cover by Tim Hartsfield

(Illustration 1) Standing in the clouds, Dante watches circles of brilliant angels, shining like jewels. (Dore illustration for <u>Divine Comedy</u>.)

DO YOU HAVE A GUARDIAN ANGEL?

And other questions answered

about angels.

JOHN RONNER

DO YOU HAVE A GUARDIAN ANGEL?

And other questions answered

about angels.

JOHN RONNER

Published by:

Mamre Press, Inc.
315 Riverside Place
Indialantic, Fla. 32903

Library of Congress Cataloging in Publication Data
Ronner, John, 1951-
    Do You Have a Guardian Angel?
    And Other Questions Answered About Angels
    Bibliography: p.
    Includes index.
1. Angels -- Miscellanea.
2. Questions and answers.
I. Title.
BL477.R66   1985   291.2´15   84-62980
ISBN 0-932945-37-6 Softcover

Manufactured in the United States of America

Table of Contents

4

ANGELS ARE ALWAYS RESCUING PEOPLE IN THE BIBLE. BUT DOES THAT HAPPEN TODAY?

In Bible legend, the Jewish heroes Shadrach, Meshach and Abednego refused to bow down to a golden idol, so angering the Babylonian King Nebuchadnezzar that he ordered them pitched into a fiery furnace stoked seven times hotter than normal.

So hot that the henchmen tossing the trio inside were themselves burned up. Suddenly, the king jumped to his feet, amazed: Not only were the three walking around inside unharmed, but they were joined by a fourth figure who "looks like an angel."

As the Book of Isaiah puts it, "The Lord's hand is not shortened that it cannot save; neither his ear heavy, that it cannot hear."

Indeed, in modern times, angels are even credited with leading the 1700s founder of Methodism, John Wesley, through an angry mob.

In his book Invisible helpers, C.W. Leadbeater describes how an English farmer's two small children in Burnham Beeches, Buckinghamshire, became lost in the woods.

After unsuccessful forays by servants and laborers, the search party was regrouping at the farm when they suddenly saw a large globe of rich, golden light moving slowly across nearby fields. Within the light, the two lost children were walking home.

Just as the adults raced up to grab the children, the light faded. Asked what had happened, the two children told their elders they had been wandering in the woods, crying, when a beautiful, smiling but silent lady with a lamp appeared to lead them home.

Boyd´s Book of Odd Facts by L. M. Boyd gives the startling explanation of how Londonite William Cowper came to compose, in 1799, the hymn "God Moves in Mysterious Ways His Wonders to Perform."

It seems a depressed Cowper had hailed a taxicab one evening to take him to the Thames River where he planned to drown himself. In the thick fog, however, the cabbie wandered aimlessly, finally giving up the task as hopeless, confessing that he was too lost even to get his fare back home. Emerging from the cab, Cowper suddenly realized he was smack in front of his home.

Truly, "God Moves in Mysterious Ways His Wonders to Perform."

In The Angels of God, Arno Gaebelein recalls how he once had a forboding feeling of danger on a train trip northward and committed himself to God´s hands before falling into a peaceful sleep.

The next morning, he awoke to discover that his train had, hours earlier near midnight, been flagged to a halt by a farmer. Less than five yards from that spot, a storm had washed out a wooden railroad bridge.

The farmer said he had been awakened by a voice that told him to get up. Hearing rushing floodwaters, he lit a lantern, went outside and heard the train approaching the destroyed bridge.

"We have always believed that an angel of God acted then," Gaebelein

8

said.

Raymond Moody, who researched near-death experiences, wrote about a World War 2 infantryman in Europe who watched a strafing enemy warplane dive toward the building he was in.
As a spray of bullets, kicking up dust, headed straight toward him, the soldier suddenly felt a "wonderful, comforting presence," and heard a "kind, gentle voice" say:"I´m here with you, Reid. Your time has not come yet."
Surely, poet John Hay´s work <u>Little Breeches</u> should have the last word here on angel rescues:

"How did he git thar? Angels.

He could never have walked in that storm.

They jest scooped down and toted him
To whar it was safe and warm.

And I think that saving a little child,

And fotching him to his own,
Is a derned sight better business
Than loafing around the Throne."

(Illustration 2) The visionary John of Patmos devours a book given to him by an angel whose body is wrapped in a cloud. (Duerer scene from Revelation).

DO YOU HAVE A GUARDIAN ANGEL?

A minister once joked during a sermon to his congregation: "The greatest proof that I know of the reality of guardian angels is that some of you are alive, the way you drive an automobile."
Jesus Christ implied the existence of guardian angels for children when he said to his disciples: "See that you don't despise any of these little ones. Their angels in heaven, I tell you, are always in the presence of my Father in heaven."

The hemlock-drinking Greek philosopher Socrates claimed he had a personal guardian spirit that warned him of trouble beforehand but never bossed him.

On one occasion, this never-erring spirit cautioned Socrates against turning a particular corner. When his friends ignored the philosopher, they were suddenly shaken up and knocked down by a group of pigs.

One writer compared the ancient belief that each of us gets a guardian angel at birth -- whether it be Mother Theresa or Al Capone -- in this way: "Just as kings give their children a tutor, an attendant from his own court, so the King of Heaven has given men, his adoptive children through grace, (guardian) spirits ... from His own court."

Researchers of persons who have come back from the brink of death tell how patients occasionally encounter what seem to be guardian spirits.

Near-death investigator Raymond Moody reports that one near-death victim was told by one such guardian being that: "I have helped you through this stage of existence, but now I´m going to turn you over to others."

In a 1961 issue of Fate magazine, Hope Price wrote that her guardian angel, in the form of a beautiful young girl, had appeared more than once in her life during grave crises.

When she was a 3-week-old newborn, her mother woke up in the night to find the beautiful young girl bending over her. Moving instinctively to a nearby room, she found infant Hope nearly suffocating. For days, she nursed Hope, stricken with pneumonia, back from the edge of death. During that time, a kindly neighbor asked about a beautiful girl who sometimes walked out on the porch of Hope´s house.

Decades later, in 1934, as a newly divorced mother of three small children, Hope was about to cancel an important operation for herself because a dissatisfied housekeeper had decided to quit. But the next day, the housekeeper changed her mind. She had had a dream in which a beautiful shining young girl came to her bedside and asked her not to leave because Hope needed her.

Traditional belief is that these guardians are the low men on the totem pole of the heavenly host but painstaking in their help -- even to answering requests to get up on time and obtain a place on a crowded train.

Seance communications through mediums claim that many instances of "angelic

12

help" actually stem from dead loved ones working for us (See: Are All Angels Really Angels?).

Others attribute at least some instances of angel intervention to the subconscious mind.

Whatever the case may be, as author Theodora Ward puts it, "... Some men who are sensitive to the movements within their own inner depths find there a seemingly separate personality to whom they can turn for wisdom greater than their consciousness is capable of."

Says writer Boros in Angels And Men: "We are already strangely related, even acquainted, with the angels during our earthly lives... (After death)...we shall no longer ask, ´Who are you?´ We shall probably call out in final recognition: ´So it was you all the time!"

DO ANGELS HEAL?

In April, 1973, Harold B. Lee, the 11th president of the Mormon church,

(Illustration 3) The warrior angel Michael tells Adam he must leave Eden. (1688 edition of <u>The Poetical Works of John Milton</u>.)

told a fascinating story to listeners in the Salt Lake Tabernacle:

Suffering from a deteriorating ulcer condition, Lee was flying home cross-country. Twice, he felt what seemed to him a blessing hand laid on his head. Yet each time, looking up, he saw nothing.

Just after arriving home, Lee suffered a massive hemorrhaging. Had that taken place earlier during the flight, when the "healing hand" touched his head, it would have spelled his doom.

In Joy Snell's Ministry of Angels Here and Beyond, a shining angel is described by a clairvoyent nurse as moving from one bed to another in her hospital, often laying a hand on the foreheads of groaning patients.

In one dramatic case, a young woman suffering terrible internal injury after being run over by a heavy vehicle was given up by her doctor as hopeless. Nevertheless, the psychically-gifted nurse saw the healing angel appear at the bedside, laying its ghostly hand over the nurse's physical one as she applied a cool, damp cloth to the victim's forehead.

"Be of good cheer. She will recover," the angel assured the nurse.Later, the woman's doctor called her recovery "simply miraculous."

Meanwhile, the famed Baltimore spiritual healer Olga Worral spurned the lable "miracle worker," insisting that her healing power flowed from God."

So-called miracles are a working out of the laws of God on a higher level than we understand," said Worral.

In one documented Worral case, a Donora, Pennsylvania heart patient's surgical chest scar not only disappeared after the healing, but incredibly, the pacemaker inside his chest could no longer be found by his doctors!

One of the great healing stories in modern times involving supernatural beings began in 1858 in the foothills of the French Pyrenees Mountains, just outside a French town called Lourdes.

On Feb. 11, 14-year-old shepherdess Bernadette Soubirous, whose peasant family was so poor it lived in an ex-jail cell, came upon a spiritual being in the form of a beautiful, white-robed teen-age girl. By early next month, 20,000 people were on hand for the 15th appearance of the spirit, who eventually revealed herself as the Virgin Mary.

The rocky cave area became a shrine, famous for its healing water, which draws 3-million visitors a year, a half million of them looking for a cure. By the mid-1970s, thousands of cures had been claimed, including 63 authenticated by the Catholic Church's thorough verification system.

Experimenters at the University of Naples contaminated samples of Lourdes "healing" water and ordinary water with deadly germs, then injected the different samples into guinea pigs. The rodents given Lourdes water were reportedly not affected, while those given the ordinary contaminated water died.

WHAT´S YOUR BEST ANGEL STORY IN THE SPORTS FIELD?

In 1970, the 49ers were trailing Atlanta in the fourth quarter of a crucial football game when a 49er fan in the stands, Jacob Atabet, saw something unusual.

Atabet said he saw a flaming angel about the size of a 2-story house begin to move over the field as 49er quarterback Brodie threw a pass to a running back, who masterfully dodged Atlanta defenders to reach the end zone.

Atabet´s companion recalled seeing perhaps sunlit mist but nothing more -- certainly not the "cone of light" with flames on top as Atabet described the angel.

Later, at a bar, when Atabet´s companion suggested he had just imagined it all, an exasperated Atabet spread his arms wide and playfully commanded the angel to speak.

Just then, a low, low foghorn sounded twice. "Angel," Atabet exulted. "Now I know that you care!"

The complete story is told by Michael Murphy in <u>Jacob Atabet</u> (1977).

(Illustration 4) Dante reaches the
highest heaven, where he sees millions
of angels forming a snow-white rose.
(Dore illustration for <u>Divine Comedy</u>.)

WHERE DO ANGELS LIVE?

In heaven, of course, but what and where is that?

Christianity's greatest missionary Paul of Tarsus said he knew a man who had been snatched up to the "third" and highest heaven, although he was not sure whether this was "in the body or out of the body.

"... There he heard things that cannot be put into words, things which human lips may not speak."

In Jewish legend, the heavens usually numbered seven, including one blissful plane where angels stored the heavenly food "manna" -- used to feed the Israelites during their Exodus from Egypt. One medieval tract even claimed 390 heavens.

Jesus said simply, "There are many rooms in my Father's house..."

The "many heavens" idea is backed up by some mystics. They often describe the afterlife as a series of lower to higher worlds or dimensions that a maturing soul moves through.

These dreamy worlds are part-physical, part-mental -- where just thinking about objects can change them some of the time.

There, spirits "talk" telepathically and "move" with the speed of thought through beautiful, colorful scenery created by their own memories and thoughts -- as we form scenes in dreams.

Near-death survivors as well as mediums passing on alleged reports from departed spirits describe the first "heaven" after death as glowing with light and seranaded by deeply beautiful music.

Beyond this so-called half-physical "pleasant Purgatory" lies a higher plane which is the true "heaven" of the Bible, many claim -- the next stop for ascending souls growing in knowledge, love and morality.

A Texan who suffered a heart attack in 1969 told near-death researcher Michael Sabom that he found himself hovering over a barbed-wire fence (symbolizing the boundary between this world and the next).

On one side was a "scraggly, dirty place" dotted with mesquite brush (this world). But on the boundary's other side was gorgeous pasture with horses.

Average people are said to enter this lowest "heaven." In fact, this world is alleged by some mystics to be happier than earth because extremely negative souls are segregated from it by their own choice, clustering together in "lower" regions.

In these afterlife dimensions, some speak of angel-like "bright spirits" who tutor ordinary ones. Indeed, some say ordinary maturing souls themselves eventually become "angels."

As the ancient Christian leader St. Augustine put it, "There will not be two societies in the City of God -- one of men and the other of angels. But one only."

By the way, a 1982 study by the Gallup Organization showed that 71 percent of Americans believed in heaven that year, 53 percent in hell.

Finally, the last word goes to Paul

of Tarsus: "Eye has not seen, nor ear heard, nor has it entered into the heart of man, the things which God has prepared for those who love him."

WHY DID THE CHRISTIAN CHURCH CRACK DOWN ON ANGELS IN 745 A.D.?

During the early Christian centuries, angels underwent a population explosion.

The fact that the Bible only mentions the angels Michael,. Gabriel, and Raphael by name didn´t faze angel-happy zealots, who mass produced thousands of winged creatures by:

* Attaching the angel-making word-endings "irion" and "el" to Hebrew words. For example, the Book of Enoch´s fallen angel Baradiel was birthed by joining the Hebrew "Barad" (hail) with the angel suffix "-el." So Baradiel might be expected to preside over hailstones.

* Taking everything literally: The Bible´s suffering Job groans, "Let the

(Illustration 5) A vast flock of bad
angles tours infernal hell. (Dore
illustration for <u>Paradise Lost</u>.)

day perish wherein I was born, and the
night, which said ´A man child is
conceived.´"   Presto! Lailah (the Hebrew
word for night) comes into being as the
angel of conception because Job quotes
"night" as saying a child is conceived.

* Jumbling together Hebrew letters at
random to produce tonguetwisting
heavenly names.

* Turning foreign gods into angels.
For example, the Akkadian god of disease
Nergal was rechristened the upright
angel Nasargiel, guiding Moses on a tour
of the underworld in one tale.

The crackdown on all this came in
745 A.D. when Pope Zachary´s angel-
busting church council denounced a
series of angels including Raguel and
Uriel as false and not to be honored.
In fact, the council decreed that no
angels were to be called on for help
except the three mentioned in the Bible
by name: Michael, Gabriel and Raphael.

As the French thinker of the 1600s,
Blaise Pascal put it, "We create angels,
but trouble comes if we create too
many."

COME ON, ARE ANGELS FOR REAL?

E.C. Burne-Jones once told
Victorian-era author Oscar Wilde: "The
more materialistic science becomes, the
more angels I shall paint: Their wings
are my protest in favor of the
immortality of the soul."

Angels are mentioned nearly 300
times in the Bible, 15 times by Jesus
himself. The ancient Greek philosopher
Socrates had a guardian angel he often
relied on for advice, and Joan of Arc,
who freed France of the English, claimed
she saw angels several times a week.

Yet despite almost universal belief
in guardian spirits in those days,
modern people generally avoid the
subject -- despite a vast "underground"
literature.

"The best evidence of the skeptic is
that it can be proved that the vast
majority of people have not had personal
experience with angels," writes author
Oscar McConkie Jr.

"However, the fact that most people
have not seen angels is not a valid
argument that angels don´t exist. It is
rather like attempting to prove a case
by presenting a myriad of witnesses...
unfamiliar with the facts of the case
who have neither seen nor participated
in the situation personally."

Near-death survivors and others who
often met "angel-like" beings generally
repressed their stories until widespread
publicity in the mid-1970s made such
supernatural talk socially acceptable.

My sister Susan Williams, who
several times saw the ghost of a beloved

dead aunt, "clammed up" after being mocked over her story, and I didn´t hear it from her for another four years.

At the bottom line is this: The claim that no spirit world or angels exists is at least no more provable than the claim that they do. In fact, the anti-angel view is on shakier ground, considering the mountain of circumstantial evidence, some of it in this book.

And besides, as Jean De La Bruyere put it 300 years ago, "The exact contrary of what is generally believed is often the truth."

In fact, there are thousands who would agree with the world-class scientist and mystic of the 1700s, Emmanuel Swedenborg, who wrote: "I am well aware that many will say that no one can possibly speak with spirits and angels as long as he lives in the body... But by all this I am not deterred, for I have seen, I have heard, I have felt."

(Illustration 6) In the end times, an angel with a key binds the Dragon (Satan) with chains and casts him into a pit for 1,000 years. (Duerer illustration of Revelation.)

HOW DO YOU GREET AN ANGEL?

French farmers killed two birds with one stone. They routinely greeted each other by saying, "Good day to you and your companion" -- even when the greeted party was by himself.

Madame de Bermond (1562-1628), who allegedly was on intimate terms with her guardian angel, was in the habit of saluting her heavenly spirit whenever she walked in or out of a room. In fact, she would pause at the door, letting the angel go first.

The same angel supposedly summoned for her anyone she wanted to see, including, routinely, a mother superior. Also, the angel would wake her at hours she specified by rapping on a table, according to Cobham Brewer´s Dictionary of Miracles.

WHO ARE SOME FAMOUS OR HISTORICAL PEOPLE WHO SAW ANGELS?

A strange legend about the Middle

Ages´s top angel scholar, Thomas Aquinas, has an angel protecting his chastity with a magic girdle around his loins.

Seems Aquinas´ mother was so dead set against his going into church work that she had him kidnapped and imprisoned in the family castle for more than year.

During that time, she sent a woman to seduce him, whom Thomas promptly threw out. But that night, an angel was said to have visited him, putting a mystical girdle around Thomas´ hips to ensure against further temptation.

During the 1820s, Mormon church founder Joseph Smith was visited at age 17 by the angel Moroni at Palmyra, New York.

Moroni allegedly told Smith where to dig up golden plates studded with Egyptian-style hieroglyphics that Smith was said to have translated into the Book of Mormon. Smith eventually took around 50 wives before being shot to death by a mob in Carthage, Ill. in 1844.

In our century, the great Swiss psychiatrist Carl Jung -- who believed all minds are in unconscious contact with another on a deep level -- broke his foot and then suffered a heart attack in the late 1960s.

What followed, Jung said, was a near-death experience that he called the greatest event of his life to that point.

"It seemed to me, I was high up in space. Far below, I saw the globe of the earth, bathed in a gloriously blue light," Jung wrote.

Turning away, he saw a temple, where a black Hindu in a white gown sat in a lotus posture.

"As I approached the steps... it was as if I now carried along with me everything I had ever experienced or done."

During this time, Jung's nurse reported seeing him surrounded by a strange bright glow, a phenomenon she had seen from time to time at different deathbeds.

HOW MANY ANGELS CAN DANCE ON THE POINT OF A PIN?

The top angel thinker of the Middle Ages, Thomas Aquinas, said angels are 100 percent pure spirits, having no matter or mass and taking up no space -- like a thought.

So the answer is that every angel in God's cosmos could dance on the tiniest smidgeon of a pinpoint and all of its space would be left over.

(Illustration 7) The angels Ithuriel
and Zephon search for Satan, who is
loose on the earth. (Dore illustration
for <u>Paradise Lost</u>.)

Most angel book writers assume that this question was one of many mind game riddles of subtle logic by which medieval churchmen quibbled over angels´ finer points in the Middle Ages.

However, the famed angel philosopher Mortimer Adler insists that the medievals never asked the question. In his book The Angels And Us, he says this angel cliche was cooked up by modern types to ridicule the intense speculations about angels during the Middle Ages (See "Angel Words -- quodlibet").

ARE ALL ANGELS REALLY ANGELS?

Lots of people take it for granted that helpful beings coming from the spirit world are always angels.

Yet through history, the deep honoring of departed family members as guardian spirits has been perhaps, of all religious philosophies, the most widespread.

At every mealtime, ancient Romans

offered food to ancestral spirits guarding their households. In modern China, the male head of a clan routinely makes sacrifices, including food offerings, at the graves of forefathers.

In fact, modern spiritualists claim that dead mothers, for example, often watch over children left behind, or dead spouses their bereaved widows or widowers.

In 1973, the National Opinion Research Center at the University of Chicago came up with a startling finding when its pollsters bluntly asked a representative sampling of 1,467 Americans: "Have you ever felt that you were in touch with someone who died?"

No less than 27 percent said yes. Andrew Greely, who conducted the poll, said: "Over 50-million people have such experiences; 6-million have them often."

Even more sobering, the percentage shot up from 27 to 51 among widows and widowers who reported contact with dead spouses.

History and literature are filled with examples of helpful and watchful human "angels": The ghost of Italy's number one poet Dante is said to have appeared in a dream to his son, telling him where to find a missing manuscript. In the 1700s, Methodist church founder John Wesley was having lively conversations with the dead in his dreams, he said.

In 1905, eccentric North Carolina farmer James Chaffin made out a will leaving everything to his third son Marshall -- ignoring his widow and three other sons. But he had second thoughts in 1919 and included everyone in a second, unwitnessed will, placing it between pages of a family Bible and telling no one.

Before he died, he stuffed a scrap of paper into an inside overcoat pocket, then sewed the pocket up. On the hidden paper was the note: "Read the 27th chapter of Genesis in my daddy's old Bible."

When the farmer died in 1921, son Marshall was the sole beneficiary of the only will known. But four years later, Marshall's brother James, in a series of vivid dreams, saw his dead father standing by the bedside, wearing his black overcoat and telling James to look in the inside pocket to find a second will.

With witnesses, James located the coat, the pocket, the scrap of paper and finally the family Bible with the second will. In 1925, a lawsuit centered around the new will, which was declared valid.

In our time, reports range from Peter Sellers, who said he often has talked with his dead mother, to positive thinking minister and author Norman Vincent Peale who several times has glimpsed departed cherished family members. Or my sister, Susan Williams, who, while wide awake, clearly saw the spirit of a departed aunt, who reassured her about a worry she had.

"Any person or any thing may be employed by God to do his will... And whoever or whatever is employed becomes God's angel or messenger," said Richard

(Illustration 8) Adam and Eve are cast out of the Garden of Eden. (1688 edition of <u>The Poetical Works of John Milton</u>.)

Whateley more than a century ago.

WHAT IS THE MOST BIZARRE ANGEL DESCRIPTION ON RECORD?

One candidate for the honor is a legend in which the prophet Mohammed is taken up to heaven. There, he runs into an angel with 70,000 heads.

Now, there are 70,000 faces on each head, and each face has 70,000 mouths. In each mouth are 70,000 tongues.

And, you guessed it, each tongue is speaking 70,000 languages. Inevitably, someone took a slide rule or some such in hand and calculated this out to 5-billion mouths and 31 quadrillion (31,000 trillion) languages -- versus the 2,800 here on earth.

DO ANGELS WIELD A SWORD FOR GOD?

About 2,000 years ago, those Nazis
of the ancient world, the Assyrians, had
surrounded the Hebrew prophet Elisha and
his servant with a large troop.

Elisha had been psychically passing
on Assyrian military secrets to Israel´s
king during a war. So naturally,
Elisha´s servant, seeing the army,
suddenly cried out, "We are doomed,
sir!"

But Elisha was calm: "Don´t be
afraid. We have more on our side than
they have on theirs."

In minutes, the servant´s eyes were
opened, and he beheld "horses and
chariots of fire" all around.

Not only did the Assyrians not get
to flay the prophet alive and spread his
skin on a wall as they sometimes did
with captives -- instead, the soldiers
were blinded, according to this stirring
Old Testament legend.

About a millenium later, in the
twilight years of the Roman Empire, Pope
Leo went out to beg mercy of Attila the
Hun, whose horde had surrounded the
Eternal City.

Legend says Attila startled
everybody by withdrawing his barbarians,
explaining later that he had seen two
"shining beings" standing with flaming
swords at either side of the pontiff as
he spoke.

After hearing angels´ voices, the
French farmgirl Joan of Arc led armies
driving the English out of her country
during the Hundred Year´s War -- before

being betrayed and burned as a witch.

But some of the most dramatic stories of angels on the battlefield made headlines during World War 1, as a routed, retreating British army faced annihilation at the hands of the Kaiser´s pursuing army.

On Aug. 24, 1914, a host of bizarre tales began to swirl up and down the front. A retreating British company claimed an angel troop interposed itself between the Britons and pursuing German cavalry, causing its horses to rear, wheel and stampede. Meanwhile, the British used the confusion to escape.

Elsewhere, a trapped British unit fixed bayonets for a desperate charge, shouting "St. George for England!"

Suddenly, they noticed a larger group beside them, wielding longbows and arrows. In fact, later on, a German POW complained about the "leader" of the ghostly cavalry who was such an easy target yet could not be hit.

Indeed, so many wounded soldiers spoke of the so-called "Spectral Army of Mons (Belgium)" in English hospitals that many nurses became believers.

In her book Marching Orders for the End Battle, Corrie ten Boom describes a strange incident during the Jeunesse rebellion in the Congo.

There, rebels had repeatedly tried to attack a practically defenseless school attended by about 200 missionaries´ children. Yet each time, the rebels suddenly ran away for no apparent reason.

Finally, one wounded rebel being treated at a mission hospital explained

37

(Illustration 9) At the end of the world, the Four Horsemen of the Apocalypse are released from heaven. (Duerer scene from Revelation.)

the mysterious retreats:

"We could not (attack). We saw hundreds of soldiers in white uniforms, and we became scared."

To quote Christianity's number two man, Paul of Tarsus: "In view of all this, what can we say? If God is for us, who can be against us?" (Romans 8:31)

JUST HOW BRILLIANT AND BEAUTIFUL ARE ANGELS?

A little over a century after Rome fell, Pope Gregory the Great was admiring the good looks of British slaves in Rome's marketplace. Told the handsome slaves belonged to the tribe called Angles (of Anglo-Saxon fame) -- Christendom's number one man protested: "They're not Angles, they're angels!"

Just how beautiful are angels?

Salvation Army founder General William Booth had a vision in which he saw angels cloaked in brilliant, rainbow light. Persons surviving near-death experiences often describe meeting dazzling "beings of light." But one of the most startling stories on record about the beauty and brilliance of angels goes back to 1960 and Ballardville, Mass.

There, Smith College professor Ralph Harlow and his wife Marion were on a May morning stroll through woods when they heard a muted murmuring behind them.

Looking up, they watched six young gloriously beautiful women in flowing white garments float about 10 feet overhead, earnestly conversing with each other. The angels passed on until their conversation faded out.

More than astounded, Harlow sat on a fallen tree trunk and quizzed his wife about what she'd seen.

"For those split seconds, the veil between our world and the spirit world was lifted," she remarked.

Meanwhile, in France, Father Lamy, the early 20th Century priest who regularly talked with angels, described angel "garments" as being unearthly white.

"It (the whiteness) is much softer to the eye. These bright angels are enveloped in a light so different from ours that by comparison, everything else seems dark.

"When you see a band of 50, you are lost in amazement. They seem clothed with golden plates, constantly moving, like so many suns."

Francisca, a saint of the 1400s, said her guardian angel's face was so brilliantly white that she could read her midnight prayers by its glow.

Curiously, her father confessor, who allegedly also saw the angel, said the being was no bigger than a 6-year-old child.

No wonder that "lightning-dressed-in-snow" is said to be the best expression to describe the angels.

IS THERE A HELL, AND DO BAD ANGELS OR DEMONS LIVE THERE?

Persons who have nearly died often come back saying they glimpsed a blissful world of light peopled by ordinary folks and dead relatives.

But some also say they glimpsed, on their way to the light, a dark zone halfway between earth and the light-world -- jammed with huge numbers of grey, dull, miserable spirits apparently clinging to our physical world.

These stories agree with longstanding reports of mediums and psychics that some of the dead, especially people who were greatly undeveloped morally, just don´t want to

(Illustration 10) During the War in Heaven, bad angels flee the Son (Jesus not yet born on earth) and tumble down to hell. (Dore illustration for <u>Paradise Lost</u>.)

"move on" from earth´s physical life.
Other spirits "stick around" as "ghosts"
because of different obsessions, perhaps
a busybody still trying to boss all
friends and neighbors or a soul deeply
concerned about someone left behind.

A woman dead for a quarter hour told
investigator Raymond Moody she passed a
"dingy, drab world" on her way to a
different world of brilliant light.

As she went by, the depressed,
shuffling spirits in the dull zone paid
her no mind. She said something was
"tying them down" because they seemed to
be hunched over -- possibly looking at
earthly things they had failed to do or
ought to do.

So-called "earthbound" spirits are
trapped by their own states of mind --
like obsessed or wrong-thinking people
on earth. Some are guilty, some angry,
some deeply caring about something
earthside, some insane or "shellshocked"
by violent deaths.

As the blind Puritan poet John
Milton says of Satan in Paradise Lost:
He takes hell with him in his head
wherever he goes, and cannot escape it.

Speaking of hell, though --
psychics, near-death victims, and
mystics do not "come back" from the
other side reporting the classical
flaming hell, populated by pitchfork-
wielding demons. What´s more, even this
stranger-than-pitchforks hell they do
report seems not for the average person,
who generally enters the "world of
light."

Taking a cue from Jesus, who the
Bible says ministered to dead "spirits

43

in prison" -- England's most famous "de-ghosting" churchman, Rev. Canon John Pearce-Higgins, became known for holding religious services to free up trapped "lost souls."

"One spirit whom I urged to look for the light said sadly: ´Where is the light?´ While another said: ´I don´t know where to go´ and yet another: ´I am in darkness,´" recalled Rev. Pearce-Higgins.

One of the most prominent of these stay-behind spirits may well be our greatest president, Abraham Lincoln, perhaps held "earthbound" by a tragic death and a deep love for his country.

Teddy Roosevelt said, "I see him in the different rooms and in the halls." Eleanor Roosevelt's secretary fled the White House's second floor screaming one day after allegedly seeing Lincoln's ghost sitting on a bed and pulling on boots.

The most striking of many stories came from the Netherland's Queen Wilhelmina: Late one night during a state visit, she heard a knock at the door of her White House guest room. Opening the door, she fainted when she saw Lincoln standing in the door frame.

Occultists claim, incidentally, that dedicated spirits on "the other side" work diligently to help straighten out the thinking of all woebegone "spirits in prison."

DO ANGELS ACT AS GUIDES?

In Bible legend, the angel Raphael led the young Tobias from Syria to Iran to meet his bride, an unfortunate maiden whose seven previous bridegrooms had mysteriously been strangled on their wedding night while with her in the nuptial bedchamber.

Along the way, Tobias´ angel guide told the understandably nervous would-be bridegroom to cut open a fish he had caught and keep the heart, liver, and gall for use against the demon Asmodeus. It was Asmodeus -- Raphael revealed to Tobias -- who was responsible for the murders.

The greasy combination worked. Asmodeus, disgusted by the smoke as Tobias burned the fish organs on his wedding night, fled the couple´s bedroom. The fiend took it on the lam all the way from Iran to Egypt, where he was tied up by another angel.

No less a figure than St. Patrick claimed to have been literally guided by an angel.

In the twilight years of the Roman empire, Patrick, at age 16, was kidnapped from a well-to-do Christian family in Britain and ended up as a slave tending swine in Ireland.

At one point, a supernatural voice suddenly gave Patrick detailed directions for an escape to the south of Ireland where a ship was to take him overseas.

Fleeing his captors, the man who eventually Christianized Ireland finally ran into coastal traders sailing for

(Illustration 11) Tobias is guided by
an angel. (Lippi scene from the Book of
Tobit.)

Gaul (France) with a boatload of wolfhounds.

In Quiet Hour Echoes, LaVern Tucker and Braith Brandt tell of a modern day Tobias and Raphael.

A female Pacific Union College student accidentally took a wrong bus, ending up in a huge, strange bus terminal, completely lost and frightened.

Suddenly, a Bible verse came to her mind: "The angel of the Lord encamps around those who fear him, and delivers them."

The woman locked herself in a restroom to pray. When she came out, she noticed a young man pass nearby carrying a Bible.

So she followed him through a maze of corridors and stairs to a bus that was -- astonishingly -- lettered ANGWIN. The right bus, even though seasoned Pacific Union College travelers knew that such a scheduling was an impossibility.

Not arguing with a miracle, she boarded the bus. The young man with the Bible hesitated, letting her pass to take the miracle bus' last remaining seat.

Then he walked off the bus. And with the woman's steady eyes still on him -- vanished into thin air. Like a light winking out. The Bible's Book of Isaiah says it well: "And the Lord will guide you continually and satisfy your desire with good things."

DO DIFFERENT ANGELS HAVE COLORS SPECIAL TO THEM?

Traditionally, the color crimson has been linked with the highest angels, the 6-winged seraphs or "burning ones" who are closest to God.

The next highest angels, the knowledgeable cherubs, are said to have blue as their color -- maybe because in the Bible, the prophet Ezekiel saw a sapphire stone over cherubs´ heads.

WHO´S WHO IN HEAVEN AND HELL?

Although the Bible only mentions angels Michael, Gabriel and Raphael by name, during the early Middle Ages, God´s messengers underwent a population explosion in human imagination.

Today, folklore and literature have:
* An angel (Donquel) to procure women and another (Lailah) in charge of conception.
* An angel who carries prayers up 900 heavens to God.

*   Still another who heads up Satan´s
secret police force in hell.

Here´s just part of a list that
could run to thousands of names if I let
it:Michael:

70,000 teardrops

Michael (Hebrew: "Who is like
God?") is the protector of the Christian
Church, guardian angel of Israel, and
commander-in-chief of God´s angel
armies. He led them during a war in
heaven in which Satan and his fallen
angels were driven out of the clouds.

In Moslem lore, Michael is described
as having hairs of saffron, wings of
green topaz and a million faces, each
face with a million eyes, each eye
shedding 70,000 tears. Even though he
lives in the seventh heaven.

As God´s sword arm, this "marshal of
Paradise" was designated by Pope Pius
XII in 1950 as the patron angel of
police officers.

Gabriel: Goodbye, Sodom

The angel that said "Hail, Mary" and
then told the Palestinian peasant girl
she would be the mother of the Christ.
Sitting on God´s left hand, Gabriel is
said to be the angel that destroyed
perverted Sodom, dictated the Koran to
Mohammed, served as God´s treasurer, and
will blow the final horn at doomsday.

In 1951, Pope Pius XII declared
Gabriel the patron angel of people
involved in electronic communication
like the television and telephone

(Illustration 12) Ascent to the Fifth
Circle. (Gustave Dore illustration for
Divine Comedy.)

because of his role as a messenger.

Raphael and the magic ring

Raphael ("God heals") is the traveler´s guide, guardian of youth and a topnotch healer. This ruler of the second heaven shows up in Christian paintings carrying a pilgrim´s stick, a wallet and a fish. Acting as healer, Raphael cured the Bible patriarch Abraham of the pain of circumcision undergone late in his life.

The poet Milton has Raphael eating supper with Adam and Eve in Eden.

In one Jewish legend, Raphael gives King Solomon a magic ring which the sage monarch uses to force a slave army of demons to finish building the Temple in Jerusalem.

Uriel: governor of the sun

Uriel -- associated by legend with earthquakes, storms, erupting volcanoes and such -- has a big part in poet Milton´s Paradise Lost.

There, as governor of the sun, he is tricked by Satan, disguised as a young angel, into giving directions to earth, and from there to Eden. Once there, tempting Satan sought out Eve´s ear.

Metatron the throne angel

Sitting beside God, Metatron, the throne angel with 72 names, records Israel´s good and bad deeds. One mystic said Metatron carries Jewish prayers up through 900 heavens to God.

Other selected angels:

* Mulciber: The fallen angel architect who designed Satan´s capital city in hell -- Pandemonium ("All-Demons").
* Abdiel: In Milton´s Paradise Lost, he was the one angel staying faithful to God among the minions following Satan.
* Beelzebub: One of Lucifer´s top lieutenants. In the Gospel of Nicodemus, Christ visits hades, getting permission from Beelzebub to liberate Adam and other imprisoned saints for a heavenbound journey.

IS THERE A CHANCE THAT WE MAY BE MEETING ANGELS "IN THE FLESH" WITHOUT BEING AWARE OF IT?

"Remember to welcome strangers in your home," the Bible advises. "There were some who did that and welcomed angels without knowing it." (Hebrews 13:2)
Legend tells how three angels on their way to destroy Sodom and Gomorrah

-- disguised as mortals -- stopped at the tent of the ancient father of the Hebrew race Abraham.

The hospitable Abraham gave the secret angels water for dusty feet, shade under a tree and a meal of calfmeat, cream and baked bread -- winning their favor unawares.

Is there really something to the host of legends similar to the Abraham story?

Typical of the disguised angel folklore is the tale of a mysterious 13th party-crashing guest who showed up at a special dinner Pope Gregory the Great was staging for 12 paupers 1,400 years ago.

The pontiff noticed that the guest appeared sometimes young and sometimes old during the meal. Leading him away to his private chamber, Gregory learned that the changling pauper was actually an angel befriended by the pontiff years earlier when the spirit had been disguised as a shipwrecked mariner.

In Columbus, Ohio, three middle-aged Irish women running a boarding house habitually set an extra place at their huge dining table -- for an angel.

This always startled new roomers, but the sisters had never forgotten a day years before when an angel appeared at dinner time to bless their food and boarders, according to writer Tobias Palmer in An Angel In My House.

Indeed, do angels sometimes move among us incognito -- as the powerful Russian Czar Peter the Great disguised himself 300 years ago to mix with the ordinary people of Europe?

(Illustration 13) During the War in
Heaven, the warrior angel Michael fights
the Dragon (Satan). (Duerer scene from
Revelation.)

In the Wheaton College Bulletin, Raymond Edman describes struggling times as a missionary among unfriendly natives in Equador.

One noon, Edman was drawn outside by a rattling of his gate to spy an elderly Indian woman who pointed to a gospel verse on a sign, saying, "Are you the people who have come to tell us about the living God?"

Then, in a mixture of Spanish and Indian Quechua, she prayed stirringly for Edman, his wife, and their work -- calling down God´s blessing on them.

For a few seconds, Edman was stunned. Then he quickly unlocked the gate, astonished to see that the woman had already vanished. Yet she had not had the time to go 10 yards and no other gates or sidestreets were nearby."...For days afterward, my own heart... burned within me as I recalled the prayer... There seemed to be an aroma incredibly sweet... which certainly did not come from the flowers in the garden," Edman said, wondering if his visitor had been -- an angel.

ARE ALL ANGELS CREATED EQUAL OR ARE SOME MORE EQUAL THAN OTHERS?

Angel thinkers generally believe that angels are split into increasingly advanced classes just as physical creatures -- from newt to Newton -- are divided up into more and more advanced stages.

As Paul of Tarsus put it, "one star differs from another in glory."

Over the centuries, churchmen have put angels in nine groups from fiery top-ranked "Seraphs" -- never quitting their meditations at the feet of God -- down to the earthly guardian angels at the bottom.

The top three ranks -- Seraphs burning with God´s love, many-eyed intellectual "Cherubs," and God-bearing "Thrones" -- stay always in God´s inner court, meditating on Him, who is the total purpose of Creation.

The middle three ranks -- Dominions, Virtues, and Powers -- keep the universe running mechanically.

The lower three -- Princes, Archangels and Angels -- carry out particular tasks.

Here´s a look at traditional beliefs and lore about each order:
* Guardian angels, the lowest order. Each of us gets one at birth.
* Archangels. They look after worldwide godly ideas -- like the notion of worshiping God.
* Princes. Stand guard over nations and leaders like the pope. They protect good spirits from attack by jealous evil spirits.

* Powers. They keep the laws of the universe working so that, for example, the force holding an electron spinning around an atomic nucleus is just right. Change that force slightly, let atoms fly apart, and physical life would be impossible in the new, totally different universe.
* Virtues. They draw on God´s force to work miracles.
* Dominions, highest of middle-order angels making the universe´s laws work.
* Thrones. These lowest of the angels who always stay in God´s inner court are called "bearers of God."
* The second-ranked cherubs -- often pictured as full of eyes to symbolize their great intellect. In angel lore, they are God´s record keepers. In popular opinion, cherubs have gone from being thought of 3,000 years ago as monstrous winged lions with human heads guarding ancient buildings to being drawn today as chubby winged babes on Christmas cards. Quite an evolution! In Bible lore, cherubs show up in their role as place guards at the Garden of Eden with flaming swords -- to keep the banished Adam away from the Garden´s Tree of Life.
* The top-ranked 6-winged seraphs, the so-called "burning ones" closest to God. Pie-Raymond Regamy compares them to "moths madly beating with their wings against the glass of the lamp (the divine light of God) at which they would (gladly) burn themselves."
These nine choirs of angels were suggested a few years after the fall of Rome by an ancient Christian writer

(Illustration 14) The angel Uriel descends from the sky to the Garden of Eden. (1688 edition of <u>The Poetical Works of John Milton</u>.)

called Dionysius who pulled names out of Bible verses and added an unhealthy dose of speculation.

In fact, ancient authorities never agreed on how many angel classes there are or the order of their ranks. What's more, some Protestant sects had as many as a dozen classes, including "Flames, Lordships, and Warriors."

Taking maybe too harsh a view of it all, Presbyterian Church founder John Calvin called the whole business of describing angel classes as "the vain babblings of idle men."

SOME PEOPLE SAY ANGELS KEEP A RECORD OF EVERY GOOD AND BAD DEED WE COMMIT FOR USE ON JUDGMENT DAY. IS THAT SO?

In moslem lore, each mortal is thought to be guarded by two angels during the day and a night shift of another two after sunset. These protecting spirits also record all his good and bad deeds for judgment day.

In fact, sunrise and sunset -- the

changing of the guard of these day and night angels -- are said to be especially hazardous times when a person could fall prey to demons.

In Leigh Hunt´s famous poem about Abou Ben Adhem, the hero "awoke one night from a deep dream of peace" to discover a recording angel by his bedside scribbling in a golden book to make a report on Abou to God.

When the angel asked if Abou had any suggestions, Abou thought a moment, then said: "Write me as one who loves his fellow man."

The angel returned the next night to show Abou that his name was now at the top of God´s honor roll.

There is evidence that the legends of recording angels may be true at least to this extent: That our own minds do the recordkeeping within our memories -- a perfect job of it!

In 1946, Canadian neurologist Wilder Penfield accidentally discovered that by stimulating the brains of conscious epileptics during surgery with an electrode, he could suddenly bring back longlost, richly vivid memories of decades past. Memories up to 40 years old were completely "relived" in color, taste, and so on.

Likewise, persons deeply hypnotized have performed amazing memory feats. And it´s become almost a trite expression for people brushing with death to say, "My whole life flashed before me." They mean they saw every event of their total lives in a flash when death suddenly appeared imminent.

In 1931, near-death survivor Leslie

Grant Scott put it this way:

"Suddenly, my whole life began to unroll before me, and I saw the purpose of it. All bitterness was wiped out for I knew the meaning of every event, and I saw its place in the pattern... I have never forgotten or lost the sense of the essential justice and rightness of things."

Indeed, 2,500 years ago, Pythagoras (the one with the theorum) taught that when death comes, the soul "sees, over and over again, its earthly existence, the scenes succeeding one another with startling clarity."

In short, a growing number of scientists now believe that, at least on some deep level, our minds record -- and never forget -- every "deed" and every thought and feeling. The "recording angel" is in our skull.

But why this perfect memory?

According to one controversial theory, the supposedly reincarnating soul -- between lives -- allegedly spends time deeply evaluating all its experiences on earth to build wisdom and character. These traits then show up enhanced in the next incarnation, some mystics and philosophers claim.

What's more, the length of time between a soul's incarnations on earth depends on how long the soul takes to mull over its experiences in the last life.

A great thinker like Plato, for example, might take 10,000 years whereas a medieval serf might need only a quarter century to ponder his simple life.

(Illustration 15) At the Jabbok River,
the Bible patriarch Jacob wrestles with
the "Dark Angel" before dawn. (Rembrandt
scene from Genesis.)

GIVE THE MEANINGS OF NINE OFFBEAT ANGEL WORDS.

Angelology: The study of angels.

Fioretti: A diary-like collection of times in your life when an angel intervened.

Genius: Our word for a mental giant was -- 2,000 years ago -- the name for the guardian spirit of an ancient Roman male. A Roman woman´s spirit was called a "Juno." In fact, Roman birthday celebrations honored the genius. And some scholars suspect that a growing belief in guardian spirits may have caused the custom of celebrating birthdays to become more and more popular in ancient times.

Quodlibet: Subtle mind games in which angel scholars of the Middle Ages logically debated the very fine points of angels. The most famous of the quodlibets is "How many angels can dance on the point of a needle?" Another brain teaser was: "If ghostly angels take on physical bodies when they appear on earth to mortals (like a job applicant donning a suit for an interview) -- what happens to the "body" when the angel goes back to heaven?

Angelophany: An angel visitation.

Demon: Comes from the ancient word "daimon," the classical Greek name for a supernatural being, good or bad, that influenced a person´s character. The great philosopher Socrates was often getting advice from what he called his "daimon" or guardian spirit.

Kairos: Something angels often take advantage of -- a favorable moment for God´s grace.

Angelolatry: The veneration of angels.

Tumtum: Not an antacid, but rather an ancient Jewish term for a spirit whose gender can´t easily be spotted.

DO ANGELS DO COUNSELING?

Kenneth Ring, who researched near-death experiences, turned up this remarkable story from a young man who accidentally knocked himself unconscious as he was about to commit suicide:
The man suddenly heard a supernatural male voice speaking to him as a close friend would, asking if he really wanted to die? The near-death victim said yes, his life had been

filled with setbacks.

"What about your mother? She cares about you. What about your girl friend?" prodded the supernatural voice, who the man felt was God.

Then, the young man was startled to hear the voice mention a daughter -- one he would apparently father in the near future.

Finally, the voice noted that suicide would be "breaking my laws... You´ll not be with me in heaven if you die." The victim asked what would happen instead but regained consciousness before getting an answer.

WHAT IS AN ANGEL´S HALO?

Painters often stylize the halo as a thin, luminous ring over the head or as a solid golden disk around it.

But a better way to think of it is as a field of light energy that surrounds the head and body not just of angels and saints, but of all of us, according to psychic researchers and

(Illustration 16)   Dante sees circles of
angels whirling through heavenly clouds.
(Dore illustration for Divine Comedy.)

mystics.

In fact, the German expression for "halo" is "holy shine" -- said by mystics to be the outline of a person's spirit body extending beyond the flesh.

I well remember the time some years back when a relative of mine was shocked to hear two of his small children tell him nonchalantly that they could see these so-called "auras" around people.

In recent decades, a new type of high voltage photography called Kirlian has shown up "auras" around living things -- auras varying in size, shape and color according to the condition of the object.

When living animals and plants die, their brilliant colorful auras -- photographed before death -- are said to fade out and disappear in later Kirlian "shots."

Some psychics claim to tell a person's emotional state by the color of his aura -- dirty red indicating passion, green jealously, purple spirituality and so on.

Mystics say there are four types of aura. The halo and nimbus, which are light streaming from the head; the aureola, light from the whole body; and the "glory," a combination of types.

Considering all this, an angel's ring-like "halo" would be a symbol of its spirit body of light.

Indeed, people who have "died" and returned to talk about it often report encounters with superior, supernatural "beings of light."

IS THERE AN "ANGEL OF DEATH" WHO ESCORTS
THE NEWLY DEAD TO THE BEYOND?

Recluse poetess Emily Dickinson
called dying "a wild night and a new
road."

And from primitive Polynesians in
modern times to the ancient Greek
philosopher Plato 2,400 years ago -- the
idea of guardian spirits guiding newly
dead souls through that "wild night" has
been commonplace.

Indeed, in recent years an
intriguing medical puzzle has gotten
widespread publicity: That dying
patients in their last moments sometimes
suddenly perk up and begin talking
excitedly and joyfully with alleged dead
relatives invisible to living witnesses
-- spirits supposedly coming to escort
the patient to the beyond.

Dying children, for example, have
been surprised to see "angels" without
wings.

Researchers Karlis Osis and Erlendur
Haraldsson tell of two nurses who were
shaken to see a dying 69-year-old woman
cancer victim start talking to her dead
husband, invisible to the nurses.

With warmth, the patient told him
how much she loved him and had missed
him and that soon she´d join him. She
even reached out and acted as if she
felt his hand.

"It was a frightening experience,"
one nurse commented grimly. "One of the
most startling things I´ve ever
experienced... to see someone where I´m
sure and positive it wasn´t drugs... The
expression in her face was -- I wish I´d

68

had a camera."

As the noted singer James Moore lay dying, he suddenly said in a strong voice: "There is mother!" referring to his dead mother. "Why, mother, have you come here to see me? No, no, I´m coming to see you. Just wait, mother, I am almost over. I can jump it. Wait, mother."

In September, 1919, the American writer Horace Traubel lay dying when he and friend L. Moore Cosgrave present at his bedside both noticed a point of light in the room. It grew larger, then condensed into the face of their old acquaintance Walt Whitman, the famous poet and Civil War nurse who had died 27 years before.

Soon, the smiling Whitman´s entire body materialized in a tweed jacket and felt hat he once wore, then faded away again.

Psychic researcher Walter Prince detailed the Whitman appearance in his Noted Witnesses to Psychic Occurences.

Besides dead friends and relatives standing in as "angels of death" -- plenty of evidence points to angels themselves acting as escorts to the beyond.

In Breath of God, author Emily Hahn relates a jarring tale from pre-Communist czarist Russia.

One of the Czar´s four small children sleeping one night in a palace nursery had been sick the previous day. For no apparent reason, their governess awoke with a start, immediately looking in the direction of the sick child. There, she saw the child surrounded

(Illustration 17)   Good angels lie
exhausted and prostrate after hard
battle with bad angels during the War in
Heaven.   (Dore illustration for <u>Paradise
Lost</u>.)

by a glowing globe of light. Within the light, a woman in a flowing white garment had gathered the child in her arms.

Paralyzed with shock, the governess watched the glowing woman leave the nursery and disappear.

After the governess jumped up shrieking, a guard showed up to see her pointing to what should have been the child´s empty cot -- except the child, puzzlingly, was still there, eyes closed.

But the governess soon was screaming again -- after touching the child´s forehead -- cold as ice.

Indeed, among patients skirting death, angel-like "beings of light" are often seen -- sometimes telling the near-death victim he must return to life and that the being will come for him later.

In Edward Randall´s <u>Frontiers of Afterlife</u>, an alleged mediumistic-type message from beyond the grave details how a newly slain soldier was helped by "angels of death:"

The soldier, along with scores of others, rose out of their bodies on the battlefield.

"We seemed to hear one another think," the death soldier supposedly communicated. "Soon there was a ray of light that grew brighter every moment, and then a great concourse of men of kindly faces came and, with comforting words, told us not to fear -- that we had made the great change, that the war for us was over..."

As Chrysostom put it, "If we need a

guide in passing from one city to
another, how much more will the soul
need someone to point out the way when
she breaks the bonds of flesh.

NAME SOME LEADING ANGEL DETECTIVES.

Here are four:
* Emmanuel Swedenborg. One of the
world's top scientists of the 1700s,
Swedenborg in his 50s began going into
trances lasting for days at a time
during which he claimed to be visiting
the spirit world.

He said that maturing human souls
gradually become angels in the
afterlife. But at first, after death,
an ordinary soul lives in a semi-
physical world. This world is, at least
partly, a "state of mind."

Swedenborg asserted that newly dead
souls go right on feeling and thinking
and doing a moment after death just as
they did a moment before death.

In fact, things are so similar that
some newly dead souls are "told by the

angels" that they have become spirits.

What's more, every word and deed of the human soul is revealed "before the angels in a light as clear as day."

Swedenborg's contemporaries considered him insane. But soon after Swedenborg died at 84 just before the American Revolution an ocean away, his followers in England founded a church based on his teachings. Its members number 100,000 worldwide today and have included Helen Keller.

* The blind Puritan poet John Milton, who wrote the greatest adventure poem in the English language, the angel-clogged 12-volume Paradise Lost.

Milton's encyclopedic story has good versus bad angels throwing mountains around as they fight in heaven. Kicked out of the sky, the bad angels fall for days to hell, where they build a demon capital city, Pandemonium.

Soon, Satan flies to the sun, where he tricks the angel Uriel into giving him directions to the Garden of Eden.

Once on earth, Satan goads Eve into eating fruit from the Tree of Knowledge. As a result of this sin, humankind's Biblical mother and father are driven from the Garden, uncomfortable hot and cold seasons are created by angels, and animals begin killing and eating each other and humans.

This blind poet of the 1600s -- who once visited Galileo when the church had him imprisoned for saying the earth goes round the sun not vice versa -- dictated his angel-crowded masterpiece to various secretaries late in his life.

* Thomas Aquinas, the "angelic doctor."

(Illustration 18)   The blind Puritan
poet John Milton.   (1688 edition of The
Poetical Works of John Milton.)

Three Poets, in three distant Ages born,
Greece, Italy, and England did adorn.
The First in loftiness of thought Surpass'd,
The Next in Majesty; in both the Last.
The force of Nature coud no farther goe:
To make a Third she joynd the former two.

When still a student, this greatest
angel scholar of the Middle Ages was
called "Dumb Ox" by his classmates
because he was heavyset and close-
mouthed. But his teacher Albertus
Magnus shot back: "This ox will one day
fill the world with his bellowing."
Sure enough, his Texas-sized work Summa
Theologica gives an excruciatingly
detailed description of the angel life.
*   The interestingly-named False
Dionysius, more often politely called
"Pseudo-Dionysius."

About 500 years after Christ, a
mysterious Middle Eastern writer calling
himself Dionysius examined the Bible´s
scattered mentionings of angel names --
from the cherubim angels with flaming
swords at the Garden of Eden to the 6-
winged seraph angel that pressed a
burning coal to the lips of the prophet
Isaiah. From these isolated stories, he
somewhat arbitrarily cooked up a
heavenly hierarchy of nine angel
classes: from guardian angels, the
lowest order, to burning seraphs, the
highest.

Unfortunately, this Middle Eastern
writer signed his works "Dionysius."
And ancient Christians jumped to the
conclusion that Dionysius was a famous
early Christian by the same name -- a
Greek judge mentioned in the Bible´s
Book of Acts. As a result, the mystery
writer´s theory of angel organization
was universally accepted in the Middle
Ages -- until scholars finally proved
his manuscripts were written centuries
after the real Dionysius lived.

For this reason, scholars today call

our mystery writer by the quaint names of "Pseudo-Dionysius" or "False-Dionysius."

DO ANGELS HAVE BODIES?

Certainly not physical bodies. Maybe spirit bodies.

Origen, probably the early Christian Church's top Bible scholar and author of a whopping 6,000 separate works, thought angels have substance and form.

On the other side, the medieval Thomas Aquinas, the Catholic Church's outstanding philosopher, called angels "holy minds" -- 100 percent non-material spirits.

Nevertheless, the same thinking goes, angels can take on a special "body" of their own for dealing with mortals -- solid and touchable.

The debate spills over into studies of those who "came back from the dead."

Some of those who nearly died and "left" their bodies referred to their new selves as points of consciousness.

Others said they had cloudy or mist-like bodies.

Typical of the vapor-type spirit body would be Little Women authoress Louisa May Alcott´s eyewitness description of her newly dead sister Betty´s spirit body rising from her physical body.

"I will tell it here, for Dr. G. said it was a fact. A few moments after the last breath came... I saw a light mist rise from her body and float up and vanish in the air. Mother´s eyes followed mine, and when I said, "What did you see?" -- she described the same light mist. Dr. G. said it was life departing visibly."

Writer Thelma Moss says this spirit body is generally invisible to physical eyes and "seems to be identical to the visible ... physical body. Apparently, it is weightless or very light in weight, so that it characteristically floats to the ceiling... or up into the sky."

Indeed, many hospital patients having out-of-body experiences report drifting upward to the ceiling as they watch doctors and nurses trying to resuscitate their bodies.

Curiously, the Old English core meaning of the word "body" was "dwelling" -- for the soul.

The final word on natural and supernatural bodies goes to Paul of Tarsus, Christianity´s number two spokesman after Jesus.

In a letter to Corinth, Greece, Paul wrote: "When buried, it is a physical body. When raised, it will be a

77

(Illustration 19) An angel suddenly appears to stop Abraham from slaying his son Isaac. (Rembrandt scene from Genesis.)

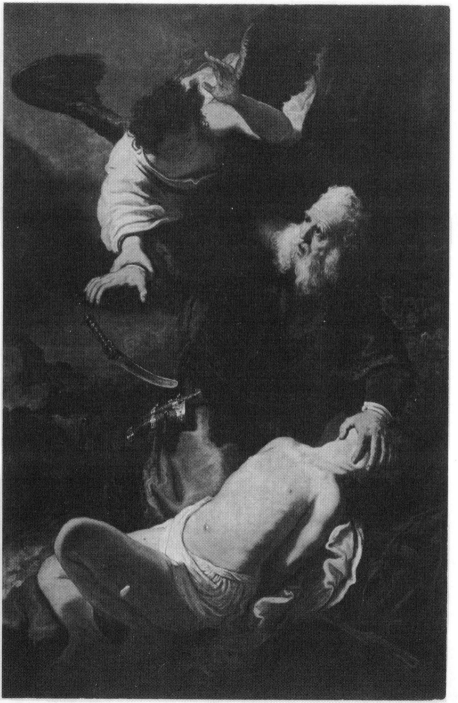

spiritual body. There is, of course, a physical body, so there has to be a spiritual body."

DO ANGELS SEPARATE NEWLY DEAD GOOD SOULS FROM BAD ONES -- THE "WHEAT FROM THE TARES?"

Jesus compared the human race to a field of wheat (good souls) littered with sometimes poisonous lookalike "tare" plants (bad souls) that grow up together. But at harvest time (death, the end of the world, etc.) -- when the tares no longer resemble the wheat, they are weeded out and burned. The wheat, meanwhile, heads for the barn (heaven).

The ancient Christian writer Pseudo-Justin put it more directly: "Immediately after the soul leaves the body, there follows a separation of the just from the sinners. Then they are led by the angels to the places they are deserving of."

Indeed, near-death survivors often mention that angel-like "beings of light" questioned them about whether they had spent their lives on earth worthily. In particular, had they learned to love others?

Yet these survivors generally say it is the soul itself that passes "judgment," not the being, who shows unearthly love and compassion.

Emmanuel Swedenborg -- the scientific genius of the 1700s who went into trances for days at a time while allegedly on out-of-body flights to the spirit world -- claimed that newly dead souls voluntarily go to the "place" that best suits their way of thinking, high or low.

"During earth-life, a beautiful body may be associated with an evil mind (and vice-versa); good people necessarily mix with wicked people. This, however, ceases... after death -- the delicate Soul Body responds immediately to every thought and feeling, and they are ´visible´ to others. In these circumstances, the wicked feel rebuked, inferior, and uncomfortable in the presence of the good: They therefore segregate themselves precisely as described by the Master (Jesus)," says psychic investigator Robert Crookall.

In fact, one near-death survivor told a researcher that, while "dead," he or she felt too embarrassed to be around spirits who had different mentalities.

Space in the spirit world depends greatly on mental attitude so that like-minded people are "close" and different-minded people tend to be as "far" as their thinking, noble or petty, is different.

The Christian writer C.S. Lewis tells a well-known tale about a busload of travelers from hell who arrive in heaven, find the place not at all to their liking, and head back home again.

"Birds of a feather" already flock together somewhat imperfectly on earth. But the noble thinker, the petty thinker, and the downright base thinker will more perfectly be segregated in the next world.

And this, by their own choice, not by angels -- the claim goes.

As poetess Emily Dickinson put it, "Who has not found the heaven below (on earth) will fail of it above."

A look at self-chosen heavens and hells comes in the story of Private George Ritchie´s brush with death, told in Guideposts magazine:

As Ritchie "died" and his spirit allegedly left his body, a superhumanly loving Christ presence appeared and filled the room with light.

After being asked by the presence what he had done with his life, he was led first on a tour of earth, where he saw miserably unhappy spirits -- "ghosts," you might say.

"People with the unhappiest faces I ever had seen. Each grief seemed different. I saw businessmen walking the corridors of the places where they had worked, trying vainly to get someone to listen to them. I saw a mother following a 60-year-old man, her son I guessed, cautioning him, instructing him. He did not seem to be listening."

Ritchie wondered if the minds of all these spirits had been obsessed with

81

(Illustration 20) Bad angels are thrown down to hell during the War in Heaven. (Dore illustration for <u>Paradise Lost</u>.)

earthly things while still alive on earth. Although no longer having an earthly life, were they still clinging to earth? "I wondered if this was hell. To care most when you are most powerless..."

Ritchie was also shown other "worlds" -- one where truth-seeking souls like sculptors and inventors worked in libraries, campuses and labs. He also saw a brilliantly beautiful "city of light."

As in so many other things, angels, it seems, leave heaven and hell up to us, both before and after death.

WHAT ARE FALLEN ANGELS?

Legend says these are the one-third of the heavenly host that, led by arrogant Lucifer, rebelled against God and were tossed out of heaven.

The Italian poet Dante has angels rebelling 20 seconds after their creation. By one bishop's count, 133,306,688 of them fell nine days to earth or hell -- depending on different stories.

According to some early Christian folklore, trouble began when the angel Semjaza led 200 comrades from heaven to earth without God´s permission to mate with beautiful mortal women.

Apparently, they were driven to that by what one ancient writer calls their "privy members... like those of horses."

Worse than the illicit sex, Semjaza´s angels taught humans all kinds of forbidden or harmful knowledge, like the vanity of cosmetics -- and warmongering.

Soon, the women gave birth to a race of gigantic hungry jacks -- one of them more than two miles tall.

These chowdowns swallowed all the world´s food, snacked on ordinary humans, and finally started cannibalizing each other.

When the earth was plunged into fornication and total anarchy, God sent down his powerful warrior angel Michael, and the lustful angels were imprisoned until doomsday in earth´s valleys.

In his multivolume epic poem <u>Paradise Lost</u>, the blind Puritan poet Milton paints a different picture altogether of fallen angels.

Here, an arrogant Satan leads rebelling angels against faithful ones defending the Mount of God in heaven as mountains are ripped up and tossed around like cannonballs.

Although the bad angels feel pain and the good ones don´t, the forces are evenly matched until the Son (Jesus Christ not yet born on earth as a man) takes the field.

The Son terrifies Lucifer´s army by hurling thunderbolts. Heaven´s crystal wall opens up to reveal a "bottomless" pit into which the panicky rebels throw themselves.

Lucifer and his plummeting angels crash land in hell and end up chained by a burning lake of fire. Eventually freeing themselves, the rebels and their dictator Lucifer build hell´s capital city, Pandemonium ("All-demon").

All told, there are as many versions of how Satan fell as there are theories of how dinosaurs became extinct or why Rome fell.

One Christian legend has Lucifer falling for disobeying God´s command to bow down before the Lord´s newest creature, Adam -- a tale found in the Koran.

In fact, ancient Christian leaders not only argued about how Lucifer fell, they also debated whether his soul would actually be saved in the end.

However, the fall was mostly blamed on an arrogant Lucifer -- the highest and most beautiful angel -- trying to usurp God´s place.

For all the colorful stories, the Old Testament frankly makes no mention of fallen angels or of battles in heaven.

What´s more, the "Lucifer" (meaning "light-bearer") mentioned in the Old Testament as having fallen is not Satan, but a figure of speech for the fallen king of Babylon, according to first-rank Bible scholars.

Whether a personal devil actually

(Illustration 21)   Dante sees Satan at
the bottom of hell, the lowest point in
the universe.   Dore illustration for
<u>Divine Comedy</u>.)

exists is debatable. Certainly, down through the ages, Flip Wilson's "Devil-made-me-do-it" idea has been applied even to monastary choirs singing off-key.

The Italian poet Dante puts a giant Satan at hell's bottommost point, caked in ice up to his chest, chewing on the world's three greatest sinners (at least in the eyes of a medieval Italian): Judas Iscariot and the two instigators of Roman emperor Julius Caesar's assassination -- Brutus and Cassius.

WHAT ARE SOME OFFBEAT JOBS CREDITED TO ANGELS?

For one thing, the ancient Christian teacher Tertullian said angels help form human embryos.

Before the time of Columbus, New World Indians already had a legend about a wandering bearded white person dressed in a glowing flowing robe and wearing golden sandals -- telling tribes about the afterlife wherever he went.

In the Old World, legends had angels bestowing all kinds of favors on pious monks. One traveling brother supposedly had a guardian angel moving ahead of him who swept and cleaned his room at monastaries where he stopped.

Some monastaries were said to get angelic kitchen help. Other angels brought food to isolated Christian hermits.

One unrestrained legend even claimed that angels transported the house of the Virgin Mary during the Middle Ages from Nazareth to Italy.

ARE ANGELS WATCHING US NOW?

Is earth a great "Superbowl" of mortal flesh where billions of tiny dramas are acted out each day with billions of spirits rooting noiselessly in the stands?

Author Vance Havner tells about a preacher who was asked by his wife why he worked so hard on a sermon he would only deliver to their small congregation.

"You forget, my dear..." retorted the minister, "... how large my audience will be!"

Around the turn of the century, the Rev. Henry Latham compared heavenly beings watching and rooting for us in our petty, earthly struggles to sympathetic parents keenly following a children´s play.

"The children gave themselves up to the illusions. They threw themselves so earnestly into their parts that their little identities seemed to be lost. ´To themselves for a moment,´ said I to myself, ´they are what they act, chiefs or pirates, heroines or (sailors), going through adventures to curdle the blood.

"But to their fathers and mothers looking on, they are nothing whatever all the time but Arthur and Harry and Ellen and Jane. What most pleased the parents was that the elder boy was not impatient with his little sister when she did not remember her part."

Likewise, angels are not so much interested in what happens Thursday at the stock market as in the honesty of the broker. Even if we take those stocks so deadly seriously.

As Christianity´s number two man, Paul of Tarsus, put it, we have "become a spectacle or theater to the world, to angels and to men."

More than 800 years ago, St. Bernard warned in a sermon: "... Whatever the corner to which you withdraw, have the greatest reverence for your angel. Would you dare to do in his presence what you would not do in my presence?

89

(Illustration 22)   At the end of the
world, angels are released to kill a
third of humankind.   (Duerer scene from
Revelation.)

Do you doubt his presence because you do not see him?"

Finally, Rev. Latham compares our "great cloud of (heavenly) witnesses" to elderly people "quitting the arena of action" to become keenly interested spectators.

"With them, objects of gratification of their own have faded away. (The old man) would like his son to enjoy all this, but he himself will stay quietly where he is. Thus, an old man is like the angels in this, that he lives by reflected happiness. He finds his main happiness in that of others -- in seeing animals and people joyous around him."

DO ANGELS, BEHIND THE SCENES, CONTROL THE MACHINERY OF THE UNIVERSE?

Lord Byron, the romantic 19th Century poet, put it this way:

"The angels all were singing out of tune/ And hoarse from having little else to do/ Excepting to wind up the sun and moon/ Or curb a runaway young star or two."

The greatest angel thinker of the Middle Ages, Thomas Aquinas, claimed that all physical things -- from orbiting planets to flowering shrubs -- are put under the responsibility of one angel or another.

In fact, one ancient Jewish writer said an angel hovers over each leaf of grass, urging: "Grow!"

The idea is that angels, working behind the scenes, run the machinery of the universe -- whose clockwork precision is still one of the greatest arguments for religion.

"Every breath of air and ray of light and heat, every beautiful prospect is... the skirts of their garments," wrote Cardinal John Henry Newman.

Some moslem mystics went so far as to believe that an angel governs each of the Arabic alphabet´s 28 letters. What´s more, the ancient Zoroastrian religion has angels called Yazatas presiding over not just individual years and months but even particular hours and separate minutes.

As for points of compass, rabbis put the militant archangel Michael over the east, the messenger Gabriel over the north, Raphael over the west, and Uriel over the south.

Incidentally, during the Middle Ages, the Protestant mystic Jacob Boehme claimed that once, while prayerfully meditating, he moved through a living, flowing light filled with colored patterns. Soon, he saw numerous spirits controlling the universe´s physical forces, according to his account.

DO ANGELS ACTUALLY SING AND PLAY HARPS IN HEAVEN?

Harp-playing is probably not to be taken literally, but unearthly beautiful heavenly music has been heard by everyone from persecuted French Protestants in the 1600s to modern near-death patients, who routinely report hearing it.

As that romantic poet of the 1800s, William Wordsworth put it -- "What know we of the Blest above/ But that they sing, and that they love?"

Indeed, some occultists and mystics, like the writer Leadbeater, have claimed that in the spirit world "all movement and action of any kind produce glorious harmonies both of sound and color."

In 1689, the Letters of Pastor Jurieu talked about dozens of cases of supernatural music being heard during a widespread persecution of Protestants in France.

In many places, heavenly music ranging from invisible choirs and ghostly trumpets to psalm singing were heard round-the-clock.

One of the most startling incidents came after a church at Orthez was destroyed. Soon, almost everyone in the town claimed to hear supernatural music, usually between 8 p.m. and 9 p.m.

Things got to the point that the Parliament of Pan and the Intendant of Bearn threatened pilgrims with fines up to 5,000 crowns from making trips to hear the music.

In the Encyclopedia of Psychic Science, where the above incidents are

(Illustration 23) An angel speaks to
Adam and Eve in the Garden of Eden.
(Dore illustration for <u>Paradise Lost</u>.)

described, Nandor Fodor says supernatural music often crops up during times of religious revival.

But this so-called "music of the spheres" is routinely reported, too, by patients who have "died" and returned to talk about it.

True, they typically begin their near-death experiences with an uncomforable buzzing or ringing sound that sometimes signals the beginning of an out-of-body experience. But that sound is temporary.

Frequently, it´s soon replaced by unearthly beautiful music.

Typical is near-death researcher Kenneth Ring´s report on a woman in her mid-30s who allegedly left her body during an intestinal operation.

The now disembodied patient saw her physical body from a distance, then soon found herself in a "pleasant valley" where she met her dead grandfather, all the while hearing "awesome" spiritual music. In fact, she later wrote a poem about the experience.

No wonder Shakespeare had Hamlet tell Horatio: "Good night, sweet prince. And flights of angels sing thee to thy rest."

IF ANGELS REALLY EXIST, WHAT DOES THAT MEAN TO ME?

An English monk of the 700s, the "Venerable Bede," wrote about the head of an English clan who "died" from an illness, then panicked his weeping relatives by suddenly reviving.

Promising to change his lifestyle, the man gave up all his property and went into a monastary. He never discussed what happened during the time he was "dead" unless the listener was serious about spiritual growth.

But to the conscientious ones, he revealed that he had met a "handsome man in a shining robe" who guided him through a valley and darkness into bright light -- to the top of a wall. From up there, the guide showed him a brilliant meadow on the other side dotted with happy spirits and mentioned that if the man lived virtuously, he would one day enter that happy land.

Modern near-death survivors often return to life saying that they, too, encountered brilliant supernatural beings who stressed to them the need to learn to love others and amass knowledge, suggesting that these two pursuits go on in the afterlife as the soul develops.

For example, one such survivor saw his whole earthly life, good and bad, flash before him as an angel-like being looked on. The being asked the person if he could love others despite their faults as he was being completely loved at that moment.

Survivors tend to "return" with a

missionary fervor to make their lives count by loving and serving others.

What's more, having seen that death is really a "dawn upon black waters," in the words of one doctor -- survivors not only lose any fear of death, many resist the idea of returning to earth at all. All this, at a time when one recent survey showed 19 percent of 3,000 Americans polled ranked death as their number one fear.

But as the famous surgeon William Hunter expressed it on his deathbed, "If I had the strength to hold a pen, I would tell how easy and delightful it is to die."

(Suicide, however, reportedly brings on very unpleasant experiences, and near-death survivors virtually unanimously call taking your life a tremendous mistake. Some suicidees report their tormenting problems were merely transferred to the spirit world and if anything, intensified.)

One comforting thought is that if angels do approach us at death, we must be worth their time.

As   Latham put it, "If angels cared about me and were happier or sadder on my account, then clearly I did not count for nothing. I was neither merged in a mass, nor was I a mere waif or stray tossed up on the shore of the world. I had come into it with a business to do, which was different from anybody else's and must be done by me."

All told, the final lesson angels may have for us is that heaven stands ready to help. What we have to do, as

Jesus put it, is "Ask, and you will receive; seek and you will find; knock and the door will be opened for you."

In Vance Havner´s words, "Our primary problem is not light, but sight. Light is of no value to a blind man. Reading books galore on the subject will not reveal the angels unless our eyes are touched by faith."

DO ANGELS HAVE A SENSE OF HUMOR?

The circumstantial evidence is that God´s choirs enjoy a good laugh like the rest of us.

Near-death researcher Raymond Moody talks about one dying patient whose "soul" drifted out of the physical body on an operating table and was soon greeted by a tremendously brilliant creature of light that made the victim feel unimaginably loved and secure.

She called the luminous being a "fun person to be with" and said it definitely had a sense of humor.

Angels have a gentle, delightful,

even perplexing humor, says author Tobias Palmer in An Angel in My House.

In the words of the popular turn-of-the-century British writer Gilbert Chesterton: "Angels can fly because they take themselves lightly."

THE BIBLE MENTIONS HOW AN ANGEL BROUGHT THE EXHAUSTED PROPHET ELIJAH HOT MEALS. BUT DO ANGELS STILL PRACTICE "PHYSICAL THERAPY" TODAY?

Evidently.

In the Bible's first book, Genesis, the slave girl Hagar was chased out of the Hebrew patriarch Abraham's camp by his jealous wife Sarah. Alone in the wilderness with her weeping, thirsty son Ishmael, she cried aloud in desperate need.

An angel appeared and "opened her eyes" so she suddenly could see a nearby well of water. Then the angel assured Hagar that "a great nation" would descend from her son.

Some of the most amazing stories of

(Illustration 24) Angels in heaven.
(1688 edition of <u>The Poetical Works of</u>
<u>John Milton</u>.)

angel intervention have these "birds of god" performing "physical therapy."

In her book A Prisoner And Yet, Corrie ten Boom tells how, as a prisoner in a Nazi death camp, she carried around a miraculous bottle of vitamin fluid.

The small vial continued producing lifesaving drops for fellow undernourished prisoners until they started calling the liquid "oil from the bottle of the widow of Zarepath" -- an inexhaustible horn of plenty in the Bible.

Not until about eight weeks later, when Corrie received a secret bagful of vitamins from a sympathetic hospital worker did the little bottle run dry -- that very day, in fact.

The new bag itself turned out to be "blessed" also.

In his book Angels: God´s Secret Agents, evangelist Billy Graham recalls how during World War 2, flying ace Eddie Rickenbacker went missing after being shot down over the Pacific. Mayor Fiorello LaGuardia asked all New York City to pray for him.

After his rescue, Rickenbacker revealed that a gull had appeared from nowhere, perching on his head -- which he grabbed and killed for food for himself and fellow survivors.

"I have no explanation except that God sent one of His angels to rescue us," Rickenbacker said.

Finally, writer C.F.O. Dell in the Dec. 22, 1955 issue of Review And Herald has this startling tale:

In a small cabin at Anchorage, Alaska, a crippled woman was alarmed to note that neighbors had forgotten to bring by heating wood for her stove.

She prayed earnestly, but the fire went out and the temperature began dropping to the 30 degrees below zero registered outside.

Suddenly, a tall, silent young man dressed in a black hat and overcoat brought in two armloads of wood to restart the stove fire.

Awestruck, the woman asked mentally if he was an angel. Instantly, the man turned around, smiled at her, and nodded his noble-featured face before wordlessly exiting.

Now petrified, she thought to herself: If that was an angel, there won't be footprints in the snow. Tottering to her door, she looked outside at a snowfield that was smooth and undisturbed.

DO ANGELS SOMETIMES SEND THE NEWLY DEAD BACK TO THE LIVING?

Persons who nearly die often report talking with a higher being -- sometimes showing himself only as a commanding voice, sometimes as a "being of light" -- about whether they should return to life.

Typical is a case reported by researcher Kenneth Ring involving a woman who hemorrhaged at childbirth but was told by a masculine voice: "You´re needed, Patricia. I´m sending you back now."

Researcher Michael Sabom told of a business executive who left his body, met his children in a place of beautiful blue color, but was told by a thundering voice to "go back" because his work on earth was not finished.

Other cases, from different researchers, describe the higher authority "allowing" a return to life because the person asked unselfishly -- for example, to help an emotionally troubled child.

Perhaps for cultural reasons, East Indians brushing with death often tell of their spirits being escorted to a commanding man dressed in white.

This well-wishing authority figure looks in a book of life and death, and not finding the mortal´s name enrolled as dead, sends the near-death patient back to the living.

Curiously, the near-death adventurers usually fall unconscious just as they actually return to their bodies, only to awake later among the living.

WHERE HAVE ALL THE ANGEL LOVERS GONE?

Like death and to a lessening degree sex, the subject of angels can´t be seriously discussed by large numbers of people in the late 20th Century without embarassment or discomfort.

True, "angel" is the in the title of every other novel or pet expression today but, as author Westermann put it, "If we listen carefully to how people speak of angels today, one thing stands out. People don´t believe in angels anymore. They haven´t believed in angels in centuries."

In fact, in the mid-1970s, evangelist Billy Graham wrote his runaway bestseller <u>Angels: God´s Secret Agents</u> after discovering just how few books on angels were in print.

Yet somebody must still care: Time magazine reported in the mid-1970s that after a TV sermon on angels preached by Billy Graham, 200,000 viewers asked for reprints.

ARE THERE SPECIAL GUARDIAN ANGELS OF COUNTRIES, POPES AND PRESIDENTS, AND SO ON?

Yes, according to the general view of believers.

Valencia, Spain has celebrated special feast days in honor of its guardian angel, for example.

In fact, Peter Lefevre was in the habit of saluting the guardian angel of each parish he visited to guard him against ambushes by heretical enemies.

Jewish lore had it that not only did Israel have the warrior angel Michael as its national guardian, but each gentile nation boasted a special guardian, too.

As for churches, the ancient Christian scholar Origen said, "One might say... that there are two bishops in each church, one visible, the other invisible, and that both are busied with the same task."

Some occultists believe that it is

(Illustration 25) Having tempted Eve to eat the forbidden fruit, the serpent slinks away. (Dore illustration for <u>Paradise Lost</u>.)

actually ethical human spirits who are what we call "guardian angels" in the spirit world. Yet these occultists also believe in special higher guardians.

According to this view, a spirit helper, with more experience, graduates up from guiding just individuals to handling groups, presidents and nations.

WHY CAN'T ANGELS BE SEEN?

In the Bible's Book of Numbers, the soothsayer Balaam is on his way to put a curse on Israel when his donkey twice leaves the roadway rather than continue. A third time, it just lies down.
Each act of stubborn resistance brings a beating from Balaam until the magician's eyes "are opened" to see a defiant angel blocking his way, meaning to kill him had he not stopped. The donkey saved Balaam's life by seeing what he didn't.

So why can't angels generally be seen?

For one thing, physical eyes are not built to see the spirit world any more

than our ears are designed to hear an
ultrahigh frequency dog whistle.

Indeed, patients whose spirits
allegedly left their bodies when they
nearly died report that their ghostly
forms were invisible to persons still
alive. In fact, their spirit bodies
passed through the flesh of the living
when physical contact was tried.

Typical of this "invisibility
predicament" is an ancient celtic legend
about two students who agreed that
whoever died first would try to contact
the other. When one did die, the other
got no visit. Finally, the second
student struck his head on a door frame,
and his spirit temporarily vacated the
physical body, meeting up with his dead
friend.

The dead friend was promptly chided
for violating their agreement, but the
ghost shot back:

"I have come many times and would be
beside your pillow pleading with you,
and you did not hear. For the dense,
heavy body does not hear the light...
(airy) soul."

According to the legend, the student
suffering the door jamb mishap
eventually returned to his physical body
to tell the tale.

Another reason for angels usual
invisiblity is that if people don´t
expect to see something, they usually
won´t -- whether it´s a cherub or a
coming bankruptcy for a failing
business.

Ordinary people who see angels are
like the Italian Renaissance sculptor
Michaelangelo, who spotted a jagged rock

and remarked to bystanders: "In that rough black rock, my friends, I see an angel. And I mean to set him free."

Is it a big surprise that in a materialistic culture that scoffs at angels, usually it´s only small children and mystics that see angels -- while the rest of us just see Michaelangelo´s rock? As Christian Morgenstern put it, "All secrets (angels included) lie before us in perfect openness." We just harden ourselves against them by degrees " from stone to seer.
"There are no mysteries as such, only uninitiated of all degrees."

HOW DO YOU SUMMON AN ANGEL?

Meeting and getting a guardian spirit was often one of the most important events in many an Indian´s life.

To summon them, young Indians often were sent out at puberty naked into the wilderness to fast and endure ordeals until a guardian spirit appeared who then stuck with them.

Their technique here was to greatly stress the mind and body until "otherworldly" visions began -- a method often used by mystics.

Another way to hail an angel, some occultists allege, is to color coordinate your warddrobe. According to this somewhat farout idea, soft green clothes will lure in guardian angels of the home, and deep sapphire blue will get the attention of healing angels, for example.

Magic buffs over the centuries have used special incantations and hocus pocus to try to conjure up special angels for everything from converting heathens (Pahaliah´s job) to procuring women (Donquel´s).

A Polish proverb, however, is more fatalistic: "In these days, you must go to heaven to find an angel."

But maybe Tobias Palmer has the most straightforward suggestion for summoning angels -- saving us the wilderness ordeal, strategically colored clothes, and incantations.

"Angels enter our lives at the invitation of our spirit," he says simply.

PEOPLE TALK ABOUT THE TREMENDOUS "SPIRITUAL POWER" OF ANGELS? WHAT´S THAT?

Suppose you tell a friend that he´s been an angel. You mean that he´s shown you superhuman goodness. Displayed greater than normal "spiritual power."

In fact, persons who have encountered superhuman "beings of light" during near-death experiences report being lost in an overpowering love and acceptance.

In a typical case, a woman whose heart stopped during an operation reported encountering a circular light that enveloped her with total, supernatural love and peace. It was, she told magazine writer Mary Ann O´Roark, a love free of any negative feelings like guilt or fear.

She interpreted this superior creature of light as God. Others have called similar beings Jesus, an angel, or simply a "being of light."

About 500 years ago, the teen-age peasant girl Joan of Arc donned armor, mounted a horse and swept France free of English soldiers after talking to angels.

"I saw them with my bodily eyes as clearly as I see you. And when they departed, I used to weep and wish that they would take me with them," said Joan.

One modern near-death survivor bluntly said he never wanted to leave the presence of the being of light he encountered.

Indeed, a glimpse of the spirit

world "and its messengers often outshines everything else for which they (the dying or near-dead) care," report researchers Karlis Osis and Erlendur Haraldsson.

Ironically, Jesus expressed that very idea 2,000 years ago:"...The kingdom of heaven is like a merchant in search of fine pearls who, on finding one pearl of great value, went and sold all that he had and bought it."

DO ANGELS GET PHYSICAL?

Is there a kernel of truth in the Bible legend that has that ancient Israelite Jacob wrestling in the predawn darkness with an angel at Penniel, trying to force the supernatural creature to bless him before releasing it?

In his Dictionary of Angels, top angel scholar Gustav Davidson recalls a time when a supernatural being got physical with him.

"At this stage of the (angel

research) I was literally bedeviled by angels. They stalked and leagured me by night and day..."

At dusk one winter's day, Davidson said he was cutting across an unfamiliar field on his way home from a neighbor's farm when suddenly "a nightmarish shape loomed up in front of me, barring my progress."

For a moment paralyzed, Davidson finally fought his way past the "phantom."

"The next morning I could not be sure (no more than Jacob was when he wrestled with his dark antagonist at Penniel) whether I had encountered a ghost, an angel, a demon, or God."

Davidson concluded that powers beyond our understanding such as angels may well exist.

An intriguing story out of Glendale, Calif. in Leslie Miller's All About Angels describes how an advertising employee was "manhandled" by a spiritual force.

An advertising executive told how an employee in his department had abandoned his wife, stolen petty cash and left in his wake a "network of lies."

The executive and the man's wife prayed together for his return.

Meanwhile, some distance away, the man was suddenly seized by the neck by an invisible, irresistible force and brought back home. It was the beginning of a complete spiritual turnaround for the returnee, who became a committed family man and dedicated worker.

"Angels can be very strong and tough in their service to us. They often

challenge us and confound us and startle
us and even knock us about... They pound
upon our lives when our lives have gone
to sleep," says writer Tobias Palmer.
    Certainly, angel legend and folklore
abound with angels getting physical.
    The reports range from cooking
angels in a Franciscan monastary to St.
Francis of Rome, who allegedly received
a "light blow heard by all" from her
guardian angel when he was displeased
with her.

HOW DO ANGELS USUALLY TALK TO US?

Harriet Beecher Stowe, the 1800s author
of slavery-busting Uncle Tom's Cabin,
answered the question in verse:
    "Sweet souls around us watch us
still/ Press nearer to our side/ Into
our thoughts, into our prayers/ With
gentle helpings glide."
    That sudden surge of confidence,
flash of insight, sharp twinge of
conscience -- may sometimes be coming
from a subtly-working angel, believers

(Illustration 26) In the end times,
four angels stop the winds from blowing
as other angels mark foreheads of the
144,000 people. (Duerer scene from
Revelation.)

say. From, as Abe Lincoln put it, "the better angels of our nature."

Writer Theordora Ward tells us how a "highly intelligent, well-educated American woman" of her acquaintance once was "emotionally paralyzed" and torn by conflict over a crucial decision.

Suddenly, she saw, standing in front of her, an angel in shining white robes stretching out his hands helpfully. Immediately, her tension eased, and the answer she needed dawned without any doubt "as if from a power beyond her knowledge or control."

In 1742, at the time London composer George Handel wrote the inspiring score of The Messiah including its stirring Hallelujah Chorus, he said, "I did think I did see all heaven before me and the Great God Himself."

Much more often than in the above cases, angels are said to invisibly plant their guiding suggestions and inspirations as "hunches," or "gut feelings" -- always careful only to suggest, not dictate to the ones they stick by."

The Creator does not abandon creatures when he has made them exist," explains Pie-Raymond Regamy.

Or in the words of that puritan of the 1600s, Harvard College President Increase Mather, "Angels both good and bad have a greater influence on this world than men are generally aware of."

HOW DO ANGELS ACT AS COMFORTERS?

A Christian legend about the martyr Lawrence has it that he was released from the torture rack when one of his captors, the Roman soldier Romanus, saw a "most beautiful young man" standing beside the victim, wiping away his blood and sweat.

"Angels are strong when we are weak and help us when we cannot help ourselves. So the financial backer of a Broadway play is called an angel -- without him the play can´t go on," said writer Ann Cameron.

Christian author Hope Friedmann tells of a comforting angel´s 5 a.m. visit:

One summer, a grieving Mrs. Friedmann was separated by great distance from her 8-year-old son Kent, suddenly stricken with polio. After deep prayer over the crisis, she fell into an exhausted sleep.

Suddenly, at 5 a.m., she awoke to see a comforting "Presence" in a soft white garment, standing beside her bed. The Presence bent over her, saying gently: "I have taken care of everything, and all is well. Do not worry." Then it vanished.

The following morning, Mrs. Friedman learned that Kent had died at 5 a.m. She said: "I understood. Though I had not reached him in time, Kent had not been alone."

WHAT IS THE EARLIEST MENTION OF ANGELS IN HISTORY?

Remember Ur? That ancient Middle East city that the Bible character Abraham, the forefather of the Jewish nation, left thousands of years ago on his way to the Promised Land in Palestine?

There, in that city more than 4,000 years old, archaelogists have found an engraved stone which some scholars think is the earliest depiction of an "angel" yet discovered.

The engraving shows a winged being coming down from heaven to pour the "water of life" from an overflowing jar into a cup held by a king. Historians know that each family in that ancient city had a personal godling who acted as the family´s spokesman during the deliberations of the greater gods in heaven.

In fact, every house kept a small chapel in honor of its "angel" or guardian spirit -- who could also take the form of a human being.

WHY DO PEOPLE SEE ANGELS IN SO MANY DIFFERENT FORMS? AS JESUS, GOD, OR EVEN HINDUISM´S LORD KRISHNA?

The confusion was summed up by Caeser´s assassin Brutus when Shakespeare had him say to a spirit he saw: "Art thou some god, some angel, or some devil?"

Why does a Christian having a vision -- say, during a brush with death -- see a powerful supernatural being he calls Jesus, while a Jew may simply see an angel, or a Hindu witness Lord Krishna?

Near-death researchers tend to agree that the superior supernatural beings which patients encounter are generally the same beings -- brilliant and unearthly loving figures of light. But patients tend to interpret what they see according to personal religion.

Secular people sometimes just describe their visions as "beings of light."

As a 54-year-old ex-mechanic told researcher Michael Sabom: "I was with an angel or God or somebody that I had total harmony with... Somebody else will have to name my companion..."

The Christian church has a centuries-old belief that angels assume special bodies when they come to earth, which one modern scholar compared to a man renting a tuxedo to be attired appropriately for a gala event.

Angels, some say, can appear as we expect them to, in firefighter´s suspenders or in a top hat and jeweled sash. They even speak our lingo: One near-death victim was told by an awesomely compassionate being of light -- "You really blew it this time."

A fine example of confusion in identifying what may be angels is Diana Powellson´s account of what happened when she nearly died in childbirth in 1876 and her soul visited a world of beautiful spirits, where some were brighter than others.

"I was much surprised when I first went there at seeing a spirit which I took to be God, and I afterwards supposed it was Jesus Christ, but (it) was only a bright spirit teaching the others. I saw many such (brighter spirits) afterwards; they don´t seem to belong to the rest at all. Everybody is engaged in learning and growing brighter, so they told me."

DO ANGELS HAVE BEARDS?

Usually not. Early Christian artists generally showed them as wingless youths.

And in recent centuries, angels have

often turned up on canvas as effeminate young males, women, and children -- but rarely as rugged he-men.

Typical is Rembrandt´s 300-year-old painting of the Bible wizard Balaam´s donkey frightened by an angel Balaam himself could not see. The portrait shows an almost unisex angel.

Consider even the exceptions, like 19th Century artist John Martin´s strongly masculine angels Xaphan and Ithuriel confronting a scowling Satan at the Garden of Eden where he was caught whispering temptation into sleeping Eve´s ear. Even that portrait shows all players still beardless.

The most extreme artistic tradition of all has turned angels into "cherubs" -- pudgy, winged babies tooting long, thin silver trumpets on Christmas card covers, for example.

One wag had a different reason for beardless angels than artists´ feminizing traditions:

"You never see angels with beards because men who get to heaven make it only by a close shave."

HOW DO ANGELS PERFORM MIRACLES?

The popular idea is that a miracle is a wonder that defies natural laws. But others have argued for centuries that miracles may actually be just the workings of higher, still-undiscovered laws.

Did Jesus tap into these higher laws when he raised the synagogue official Jairus´ daughter from death or healed lameness and leprosy? Do angels do the same?

As the English minister Maurice Elliott put it, "Yesterday´s miracles are today´s natural law."

Indeed, a 1978 Gallup Poll showed that 51 percent of American adults that year believed in the reality of psychic phenomena -- 64 percent of the college-educated. More startling was a 1972 poll by the well regarded British magazine New Scientist. Not only did 88 percent of respondents think psychic research was kosher, a surprising 25 percent called ESP a fact.

In a recent ESP experiment in Princeton, a particular subject repeatedly beat odds of 1,000 to 1 by so often correctly guessing the motion of enemy space ships in a video game cleverly called "Psi-trek."

The Soviets are said to spend at least $50-million a year on psychic research. In a 1975 U.S. experiment on clairvoyent spying, one psychic reportedly was able to give a detailed description of a clandestine, subterranean American military installation.

Yet -- as the Episcopal priest William Rauscher, past president of Spiritual Frontiers Fellowship has lamented -- the modern church has largely ignored parapsychology.

This, despite the fact that parapsychology has been called the "basic science of religion." It is to religion what biology is to medicine and what physics is to engineering, some believe.

Diehard skeptics might well consider the words of Shakespeare's Hamlet to an acquaintance:

"There are more things in heaven and earth, Horatio, than are dreamt of in your philosophy." (Said after Hamlet had spoken with his murdered father's ghost.)

DO GOOD ANGELS FIGHT EACH OTHER?

In the Old Testament, the Hebrew prophet Daniel's protective angel having a face "as bright as a flash of lightning" appears to him.

Speaking in a voice "like the roar of a great crowd," the angel, presumably Gabriel, tells Daniel that he, Gabriel, and the archangel Michael -- the guardian angel of Israel -- are locked in a fight with the guardian angels of the Persian Empire and Greece.

What puzzles theologians about this legend is that high-minded angels are fighting among themselves -- none of them seems to be a devil.

Pagans shared this notion. The ancient Greek historian Plutarch reports that during the second Roman Civil War just before Christ´s birth, an Egyptian fortune-teller made a bold prediction: That Cleopatra´s lover General Marc Anthony would be defeated by his rival, the future emperor Augustus, because Anthony´s guardian angel was weaker than Augustus´.

The great medieval religious thinker Thomas Aquinas felt that reasonable angels, like reasonable men, could differ about God´s will.

Good angel "conflict," Aquinas suggested, might actually be only a pleading before God of the best cases of hostile nations by their guardian angels -- like attorneys in a court suit.

(Illustration 27) An angel visitor
approaches at the Garden of Eden. (Dore
illustration for <u>Paradise Lost</u>.)

JUST ABOUT EVERY RELIGION TALKS ABOUT A JUDGMENT AFTER DEATH. IS THIS SO, AND ARE ANGELS INVOLVED?

The ancient <u>Tibetan Book of the Dead</u>, a "how-to" manual for the dying, explains that the newly dead spirit will appear before a "god of death" who has a mirror. And in that mirror will appear the succession of events in the soul´s lifetime on earth.

Curiously, the soul will pronounce judgment on itself -- not the god.

The great ancient Greek philosopher Plato tells how the soldier Er was thought killed in battle. But as his body was dumped on a funeral pyre, he came to and claimed to have been in the spirit world.

There, Er alleged, he had seen fellow souls being judged by divine beings who could, in a quick glance, see everything the soul had done on earth.

Modern "Ers" who have brushed with death and come back consistently speak of encountering "beings of light" or intelligent radiant "presences."

These overwhelmingly loving supernatural beings ask them about their lives while the near-death victims watch every tiny action of their earthly life displayed before them -- some say in color and 3D.

According to near-death survivors, these brilliant beings routinely stress the importance of learning to love others on earth and of developing knowledge and wisdom, implying that learning continues even after death.

Backing up what the <u>Tibetan Book of</u>

the Dead said centuries ago, these back-from-the-dead survivors recall judging themselves as they saw their lives played back, rejoicing over the good deeds, regretting the selfish ones.

Through it all, the supernatural being was said to be warmly supportive, pointing out that even the mistakes were learning experiences.

Yet some mystics claim the judgment time can be a "terrible hour" of self-judgment for above-average wrongdoers, who suddenly see the unmasked truth of their lives through their soul's much more sensitive "eyes." No more rationalizations.

In The Supreme Adventure, Robert Crookall includes the story of ex-convict Starr Daily's self-judgment-type experience when he slipped into a coma:

In what seemed like a wide-awake dream, Daily watched what looked like a motion picture film, seeing a "vast number" of people he had injured directly and hundreds more hurt indirectly. Plus scores of others suffering still smaller injuries by his "thoughtless words and looks and omissions."

"The most terrifying thing about it was that every pang of suffering I had caused others was now felt by me..." he added. But Daily at least was next able to view his good deeds.

Besides self-judging the good and evil in his life, the near-death survivor is often asked by the being of light if he wants to return to life or is told he must do so -- sometimes with a brief description of what his future holds.

Who is this supernatural being that helps the soul to judge itself -- for the purpose of improving the soul´s character, some mystics say.

Christians sometimes call the being Jesus or God, some Jews have used the word angel, while secular people simply say "presence" or "being of light." The labeling seems to depend on religious background.

Finally, let´s give the last word to the Koran: "When a man dies, they who survive him ask what property he has left behind. The angel who bends over the dying man asks what good deeds he has sent before him."

HOW DO ANGELS THINK?

For one thing, angels need fewer mental concepts to understand the world than we do -- just as a genius draws more conclusions from the same facts than a dullard.

As a matter of fact, the higher the

angel, the fewer concepts he needs to understand the universe because those fewer ideas are more far-reaching. Finally, there is God Himself, Who understands everything with a single all-embracing thought.

Think of Newton, for example. When the legendary apple fell on his head, he did not say, as we would have, "There goes another apple."

Understanding much, much more from this single fact, his genius´ mind came up with the law of gravity.

As author Daphne Mould put it, "The higher an angel (in the series of better and better minds leading up God Himself), the fewer concepts he needs to understand the world, just as more powerful human minds grasp a range of conclusions from a few general principles while the more stupid of us (understand) only a scatter of isolated events and facts."

By the way, a common opinion of the Christian church, neither proved nor disproved, is that all angels sprang into being with their storehouse of knowledge built in.

ARE THERE RACES OF ANGELS?

The Middle Ages´ number one angel thinker, Thomas Aquinas, believed that each angel is so different from every other angel, that it is a separate species.

"... One angel, in its fullness of being, is as distinct from another as one universe from another" -- as Pie-Raymond Regamy put it.

But there are dissenters, like the famous Scottish philosopher of the 1200s Duns Scotus (from whose name comes our word "dunce") who thought that all angels belong to the same species.

Others take a middle ground: that there are "many" species.

A parting thought from America´s John Adams: "Nature, which has established a chain of being... descending from angels to microscopic animalcules, has ordained that no two objects shall be perfectly alike, and no two creatures perfectly equal."

WHEN PEOPLE DIE, DO THEY INSTANTLY BECOME ANGELS, GRADUALLY, OR NOT AT ALL?

At a church graveyard in northern Wales, a tombstone for 8-year-old Richard Jebb, who died in 1845, reads:

"Rest, gentle Shade/ Await thy Master´s will/ Then rise unchanged/ And be an angel still."

Nevertheless, the popular idea that people instantly get halos at death is thought wrong by both orthodox churchmen and mystics.

As Treasure Island author Robert Louis Stevenson put it, "To equip a dull, respectable person with wings would be but to make a parady of an angel."

Traditional Christians usually think of angels as a separate "species" of beings made before humankind was even created. For mortals to "earn their wings" by dying would be like a parrot going to sleep and waking up an eagle.

Many mystics, however, see human souls constantly growing in knowledge, ethics and wisdom until they gradually become ordinary, then higher and higher angels.

In the words of Longfellow, the 1800s poet: "Where´er a noble deed is wrought/ Where´er is spoken a noble thought/ Our hearts in glad surprise/ To higher levels rise."

In 203 A.D., the night before she was sentenced to die in a Roman arena, the Christian martyr Perpetua had a dream symbolic of the soul´s struggle upward to the angel world.

In her dream, she saw an incredibly

long, thin brass ladder stretching from earth to heaven -- flanked by daggers to cut the flesh of a climber who was careless (in building a strong character?). Below the ladder was a giant dragon waiting for those who fell, trying to frighten the climbers.

Once she struggled upward to heaven, she spotted a white-haired shepherd milking sheep, surrounded by thousands of white-clad persons. The shepherd raised his head and said: "You have come well, my child."

The following morning, Perpetua faced a crazed heifer in the arena so bravely, she was allowed to die by sword. And when the young executioner hesitated, she grabbed his hand and led it to her throat.

A final thought on the evolution of the soul: Some researchers into the brain think that empathy -- a compassionate feeling for other creatures and their situation -- is the main job of the so-called prefrontal cortex, the brain's most recently evolved section.

One of the world's greatest mystics, the genius scientist of the 1700s, Emmanuel Swedenborg, said flatly: "Angels are human forms, are men, for I have conversed with them as man to man."

CAN ANGELS HELP US WITH PRAYER?

One legend says the angel Metatron carries prayers up through 900 different heavens to God.

If the prayer is in Hebrew, says a different legend, the same Metatron teams up with angels Achtariel and Sandalphon to weave a garland out of it.

Like backbenchers "amening" the preacher in a country church, the guardian angel prays along with his earthling protege.

But traffic is 2-way. Besides beefing up prayer, angels "also bring God´s messages to our souls, feeding them... with delightful inspirations and communications from God..." according to St. John of the Cross.

WHAT ARE SOME ANGEL NICKNAMES?

Dante, Italy´s number one poet, called them "birds of God," while Lactantius referred to them as "breaths of God."

In the Bible, they are variously
dubbed "sons of God," "Meditators,"
"Hosts," and "Holy Watchers."

WHAT DO ANGELS WEAR?

Being pure spirits, they wear
nothing. But they will appear to
mortals "wearing" whatever´s expected,
from a policeman´s uniform to a
handlebar moustache and monocle.

That´s why most people see a long
white robe bound at the waist -- just
what most often is expected.

Interestingly, Christian artists are
in the habit of picturing angels as
barefoot, though archangels are often
deferentially given sandals.

(Illustration 28) At the end of the
world, a seven-headed dragon appears.
(Duerer scene from Revelation.)

DID THE PAGANS OF OLDEN TIMES HAVE ANGELS, TOO?

Of course. Ancient religions had hordes of minor godlings greater than mortals but lesser than bonafide deities.

For example, guardian angels would have their parallel in ancient Rome's "Lares" -- protective household gods who were offered food at every meal. The head "Lar" was the spirit of the family's founder.

Angels of death, escorting the newly dead to the beyond, do the work that a Viking would expect of the "valkyries."

These horse-mounted supernatural maidens scooped up slain warriors from the battlefield and hauled them up to head god Odin's beer hall in the clouds, "Valhalla."

In a curious parallel to dying persons who often spot angels or deceased relatives in their last moments -- legend has it that a warrior's sighting of a valkyrie on the battlefield meant his imminent death.

As for the messenger angel, one of many parallels is the Greek god Hermes, flitting to and fro on winged sandals.

WHAT ARE THE MOST FREQUENTLY ASKED QUESTIONS ABOUT ANGELS?

Philosopher Mortimer Adler said that during the year he spent writing his book The Angels And Us, nearly everyone he told about the project had two specific questions: "Do you believe in angels?" and "How many can stand on the head of a pin?"

HOW DO ANGELS MOVE AROUND?

Not like us. Consider the closest thing to an angel on earth -- your mind or soul.In the blink of an eye, your mind -- which is spirit like an angel -- can go from the room you were married in to the edge of the universe.

Being spirits, angels move like our imaginations -- instantly, as near or far as they want, to the past, present or future.

Indeed, mortals having so-called out-of-body experiences -- where the mind or soul allegedly leaves the body

-- routinely report that travel becomes instantaneous and unlimited.

"...by a mere splitsecond thought, I could travel millions of miles," reported one psychic traveler.

Said another: "All movement was instantaneous. To think was to have acted."

Author Peter Wilson tells of an older Canadian Indian´s reaction to news that humankind had landed on the moon.

"Oh, that´s nothing. My uncle went to the moon plenty of times," he said, referring to an out-of-body flight such as medicine men, African witch doctors and the like have claimed to be making for thousands of years.

Helen Keller claimed to have left a library "mentally" for a visit to Athens, Greece.

In 1774, when the American Revolution was stirring over here, a prisoner in Italy named Alphonse de Liguori became quiet in his cell and took no food for five days. When he awoke, he claimed to have been at the deathbed of Pope Clement XIV.

Remarkably, Liguori was indeed witnessed in the pope´s chamber -- perhaps the Catholic Church´s most famous case of what it calls "bilocation."

When angels are not flitting around with the speed of thought, do they take up space?

Philosophers say they don´t, being nonphysical spirits. Rather, an angel is where it applies its power and influence, they say.

Of course, nonphysical angels are

expected to be able to pass through physical things like walls.

And in fact, people claiming out-of-body flights report the same thing.

A 33-year-old Vietnam vet who lost two legs and an arm in a mine explosion told near-death researcher Michael Sabom that when he left his body, he discovered he could not grab hold of the doctors performing lifesaving surgery on the body he left behind.

What happened when he tried?

"Nothing... I grabbed, and he (the doctor) wasn't there or either I just went through him or whatever."

WHERE ARE YOU MOST LIKELY TO MEET AN ANGEL?

Where everything else isn't -- an isolated place where sitcom laugh tracks, backfiring auto engines and other physical distractions can't drown out the supernatural.

Before starting his ministry, Jesus spent 40 days in the quiet wilderness where "angels came and helped him."

The ancient Christian hermits of the late Roman Empire spent years in the wilds fasting and meditating in isolation, in part to get in closer touch with the supernatural world.

Some extremists went so far as to live in snake-infested swamps. One of the most extreme of the extremists, Simeon Stylites, sat atop a 60-foot-high pillar alone for 30 years.

Indeed, there is evidence that long isolation causes a changed "state of consciousness" that can bring on supernatural visions.

Consider Call Of The Wild author Jack London´s 1918 novel called Star Rover. The book had its basis in the alleged out-of-body trips his friend Ed Morrell took during the half decade when Morrell was in solitary confinement at San Quentin prison.

When Admiral Byrd was in complete isolation for six months at the South Pole, he sometimes had the feeling -- as he lay in his bed -- that he was floating "in disembodied space."

But does this "changed state of consciousness" allow a person to become aware of angels that perhaps are actually around all the time?

In Camp Six, F.S. Smythe details how he suddenly found himself alone and in danger on Mount Everest during an unsuccessful 1933 expedition."... A strange feeling possessed me that I was accompanied by another," he wrote."This ´presence´ was strong and friendly. In its company I could not feel lonely, neither could I come to any harm. It was always there to sustain me on my solitary climb up the snow-covered slabs.

"Now, as I halted and extracted some mint cake from my pocket, it was so near and so strong that instinctively I divided the mint into two halves and turned round with one half in my hand to offer it to my companion."

Smythe's only explanation was that perhaps he was in a stressful detached state, standing beside himself, watching himself. Yet this story is similar to those of others finding themselves isolated under challenging or stressful conditions.

While crossing Greenland's desolate, lonely ice cap in 1965, worldwide explorer Myrtle Simpson became aware of "someone else with us."

"For three nights, the going was fast and fine. But ice and isolation began to play subtle tricks with my imagination," she wrote in National Geographic.

"I began to feel that someone else was with us. 'He' kept looking over my shoulder. The 'green man' of Greenland, perhaps. Roger (mountain climber Roger Tufft) confessed that he, too, had felt the strange, unseen presence."

During a calamitous early 20th Century trip back from an expedition to the South Pole, British explorer Ernest Henry Shackleton and his fellow travers reportedly became conscious of a supernatural companion who went with them.

WHY DO ANGELS GO ON HOLIDAYS?

A troublesome question for centuries has been why angels help some people but allow disaster to overtake others -- a variation on the "Why-did-God-let-this-happen" complaint.

Why do angels "go on a holiday?"

For example, an angel sprang Jesus´ disciple Peter from King Herod´s prison. But Herod was allowed to execute Peter´s fellow disciple James by the sword.

One partial answer may be that adversity teaches. A toddler won´t walk easily till he´s fallen many times. Some learn honesty by suffering the consequences of cheating others or being cheated themselves.

A more mystical -- and controversial -- claim put forward by some is that misfortune suffered in this life may be the consequence of something in a "past life."

The great philosopher of the 1800s, Ralph Waldo Emerson, saw the universe as a great echo chamber in which the good we do boomerangs back to us, sooner or later in one form or another -- and likewise the evil. Until everything balances out.

As Christianity´s number two spokesman, Paul of Tarsus put it, "Do not deceive yourselves. No one makes a fool of God. A person will reap exactly what he plants."

Still others say trouble can be brought on by "negative thinking" like hate or worry until the subconcious mind eventually -- almost supernaturally -- turns a person´s fixated thoughts into reality.

By contrast, the positive thinker attracts fortune and repels harm.

Actually, there is no clearcut answer to angelic "vacations" -- just a horn of plenty of intriguing theories.

HOW LONG DO ANGELS LIVE?

Most pundits say angels will live forever -- like the human soul, both being made of indestructible spirit.

"(The spirit) is like the sun, which seems to set only in our earthly eyes, but which really never sets, but shines on perpetually," said Johann von Goethe, the giant of German literature.

Indeed, Christian artists have often showed angels as youths to symbolize their immortality.

Although believers agree angels will never die, that does not mean they are eternal. Only God always existed. Angels came later as part of God´s creation of the universe, and, some ´ claim, before any other creature.

Pollsters seem not to ask people much about angels but there are several surveys showing that about 70 percent of the American public believes in the soul´s immortality.

ARE THERE ANY GROUPS OR CLUBS INTERESTED IN ANGELS?

In 1950, an organization to honor angels called "Philangeli" (Friends of Angels) was formed in England and soon spread as far away as Canada, India, Australia and other countries.

By the mid-1960s, the Clerics of St. Viator at Lyons, France, were putting out a publication called "L´Ange gardien" (The guardian angel).

Closer to home, the 1984 Gale Encyclopedia of Associations lists the 650-member Angel Collectors Club of America. These collectors of angel ornaments, dolls and the like present angel talks before church groups and retirement homes. Their newsletter is titled: "Halo, Everybody!"

(Illustration 29) The visionary John of
Patmos sees Christ flanked by seven
candlesticks. (Duerer scene from
Revelation.)

IS THERE ONE LANGUAGE FOR MORTALS AND ANOTHER LANGUAGE FOR ANGELS?

In the New Testament, Paul of Tarsus, Christianity´s greatest missionary who evangelized the Roman empire about a generation after Christ, spoke of their being one language for men and another eloquent one for angels:

"If I speak in the tongues of men and of angels, but have not love, I am a noisy gong or a clanging cymbal," he wrote in a letter to Christians in Corinth, Greece.

For centuries, it was assumed that angels speak Hebrew, which legends say was the tongue of Adam, Eve and even the tempting serpent at Eden -- in fact, God´s language when he created the world.

Indeed, not until God deliberately thwarted the builders of the heaven-scaling Tower of Babel by giving them different languages did Hebrew stop being humankind´s universal speech -- so the legend goes.

While some credited such linguistic angels as Metatron with a mastery of 70 tongues, others said angels can´t understand anything but Hebrew.

The whole issue got even sillier during the reign of England´s virgin queen Elizabeth 1, whose court astrologer used a medium and a magical obsidian mirror to discover that angel language is "Enochian." The name apparently comes from an Old Testament character, Enoch, who fathered the oldest man, Methusaleh, then later was swept up to heaven without having to die.

Nevertheless, serious thinkers like Thomas Aquinas, the Middle Ages´ top angel scholar, asserted that the actual language of angels is a wordless exchange of thoughts -- "illumination" to use his term, "telepathy," to use ours.

Today, the mounting evidence for telepathy even among us non-angels is typified by Upton Sinclair´s 1930 book Mental_Radio detailing the psychic abilities of his wife. The book so impressed a fellow named Albert Einstein that he wrote a preface for it.

DO ANGELS HAVE WINGS?

The early books of the Old Testament make no mention of their angels having wings -- such as the "dark angel" who wrestled with the Jewish patriarch Jacob at a river ford before dawn.

What´s more, the earliest Christian artists showed angels as wingless youths.

In fact, angel wings did not start to crop up in Christian art until roughly the era of Rome´s first Christian emperor, Constantine the Great, the one who converted after seeing a cross in the sky before a major battle.

Angels then began to take on the winged look of the ancient Greek goddess of victory Nike -- whose name today is known mostly as an athletic brand.

In reality, spiritual beings that flit about with the speed of thought probably don´t need literal wings. Still, wings are good symbols of that "rapid flight."

WHAT´S AN ANGEL´S BIGGEST JOB?

In the Bible, at least, angels show up most often as messengers. In fact, the name angel itself comes from the Greek word for messenger.

For example, after Jesus´ body was laid in the tomb, women coming to embalm it ran into "dazzling" angels with definite tidings.

Referring to the fact that Jesus had risen from the dead, these cosmic message bearers asked, "Why do you seek the living among the dead?"

A striking modern story about messenger angels concerns the Italian priest Pio Pietrelcina who suggested that people needing spiritual help or prayer senᵈ him their guardian angels -- missions that are said to have brought satisfying results to the petitioners.

An associate of the priest reported that Father Pietrelcina complained one morning that a steady succession of arriving guardian angels with different requests the night before had kept him awake all night.

LIST SOME SUPERSTITIONS ABOUT ANGELS.

Here´s a sampling:
* When a child smiles in its sleep, it is talking to angels, according to the Irish. But the Armenians say this really means that the child´s guardian

angel is tickling him by cutting his
fingernails.
* If someone died in a Latin American
or Spanish house, it was an old custom
to put black curtains over all mirrors
to keep the Angel of Death from spotting
his image in the looking glass.
* Ringing church bells are useful for
chasing away demons.

HOW AND WHEN WERE ANGELS CREATED?

The usual opinion is that eternal
God was "there" first, of course. Then
He created angels, then the universe.
And only after all that was man
produced.

You see this timetable, for example,
in a moslem legend that has Allah
sending off the already-existing angels
Gabriel, Michael, and Israfel on a
mission to earth. They are to gather up
different types of clay for Allah to use
in making Adam, the first man.

However, when the earth cautions the
angelic trio that the new creature will

rebel against his Maker and bring misfortune to earth, the three return home without the variously colored soils. But an unhappy Allah reacts by sending the angel Azrael instead, who is rewarded for a successful mission by being put in charge of splitting off dying people´s spirits from their bodies.

Boosters of a pre-universe angel creation like to cite a Bible legend in which God tonguelashes suffering Job.

"Who are you to question my wisdom...?" asks God of Job -- adding that the angels were already singing when He started to build the cosmos.

As for ideas about the how, rather than when, of angel creation, one rabbi´s quaint opinion was that an angel is created every time a word comes out of God´s mouth.

A different, mystical theory holds that because many people believe in angels, that belief itself creates angels out of God´s energy and keeps them in existence.

WHY DO ANGELS SEEM TO KNOW THE FUTURE AS
WELL AS THE PAST?

When Paul of Tarsus, Christianity´s
greatest missionary, was arrested in
Jerusalem, he demanded a trial before
Caesar, his right as a Roman citizen.

During a boat trip to Italy, in the
midst of a great storm about to break up
the ship, an angel appeared before Paul,
foretelling that noone aboard would die.

In fact, the angel predicted, Paul
would live to stand trial in the Eternal
City -- so goes the story in the Bible´s
Book of Acts.

What´s more, modern persons who have
nearly died often encounter
supernaturally powerful beings during
their medical crises who tell the
patients about future events in their
lives.

In 1978, a Gallup Poll reported that
37 percent of adults questioned believed
that future events can be foretold. The
answer to this riddle may be, as mystics
say, that time and space do not really
exist in the spirit world, at least not
completely.

In Raynor Johnson´s A Religious
Outlook for Modern Man, a woman whose
soul allegedly left her body during
childbirth put it this way:

"Next, I was able to understand that
here (in the spirit world) we are not
bound by Space and Time. Space was easy
-- just to think of a place was to be
there... Our little daughter of 2 1/2
was an intelligent, unusual, droll
child.´.. Now I saw her as a baby, a
child, a girl, a woman, and as an old,

old lady... It was as if her life were on a length of tape, not visual only, but whole and living. While one section was on view at a certain age in the physical world, here it was more like a composite picture... past, present and future."

In a study of 114 cases, near-death researcher Russell Noyes determined that 80 percent felt a change in the passage of time during their experience.

With angels, the thinking goes, past, present, and future are one. Angels can spread out the past and future before them like we unfold a map, as Rev. Henry Latham put it way back in 1896.

Typical of near-death patients and mystics claiming that the spirit world is timeless -- is the response of one woman asked how long her experience lasted: She said it could be described as either a brief moment or centuries.

WHAT DO ANGELS EAT?

The stock answer is manna -- the mysterious food raining down from heaven that the wandering Israelites ate in the Sinai wilderness during their exodus from Pharoah's Egypt.

The Bible describes "manna" (from the Aramaic expression "What is this?" because that's what the Israelites asked when they saw it.) as a thin, flaky substance covering the ground and "delicate as frost."

"It was like a small white seed and tasted like thin cakes made of honey," the Bible goes on.

In fact, Bible scholars say there is indeed a nourishing substance similar to this Bible description on low tamarisk shrubs in the Sinai wilderness and other deserts. According to one study, this "manna" is excreted by plant lice and hardens in the dry desert air.

However, manna or no manna, the idea that spiritual creatures like angels would have to eat -- a physical activity -- seems doubtful.

As one wag put it, "Many a man treats his wife like an angel -- nothing to eat and less to wear."

But, as the following startling story shows, angels do seem to humor us by eating when that's what we expect of them:

Passing out religious literature in a Philippines neighborhood, a Seventh Day Adventist missionary surprised a homeowner she called on when the resident's police dogs failed to become excited in the least as the missionary

(Illustration 30) Satan returns to his hellish capital of Pandemonium to find his bad angels have become snakes. (Dore illustration for Paradise Lost.)

showed up.

Indoors, the lady of the house, in turn, surprised the missionary by pulling out two guest chairs instead of one, then addressing the empty chair as though in a conversation with someone invisible.

At one point, the mistress of the house turned to the missionary and remarked that her "companion" looked becoming in white.

At the lunch table, the missionary sneaked a glance at a half-drained milk glass in front of the invisible visitor´s place setting.

Finally, as the missionary left the house, the mistress, seeing her off, placed one hand on the Seventh Day Adventist´s shoulder and another in mid-air, as if on an invisible shoulder.

Before coming to that house -- in a hostile neighborhood -- the missionary had prayed for protection and guidance.

The entire baffling story is told in Raymond Woolsey´s <u>Joy in the Morning</u>.

WHAT ATTITUDE SHOULD I HAVE TOWARD AN ANGEL?

In the Bible´s last book, the visionary John falls down to worship an angel showing him what the end of the world will be like. But the angel is not pleased.

"I am your fellow servant," the angel complains. "Worship God."

The whole ancient Christian church was confused over how angels should be treated, as some leaders okayed the idea of revering the beings while others scorned it as "masked idolatry."

About 300 years after Rome fell, a gathering of Christian bishops from all over the Byzantine Empire finally gave a clean bill of health to the so-called "cult of angels" -- that is, the deep honoring of angels, but without worship, to be reserved for God alone.

As writer T. Howard put it, "But of course in the city of God, it never comes to a matter of jockeying for position, or of comparing credentials or of sniffing at questions of dignity and precedence. No angel will ever quarrel with any of us about comparative dignity, and, until we know something we don´t know now, our posture in front of them had better be prone."

The Catholic Church uses the offbeat word "dulia" to refer to secondary homage to angels and saints while "latria" is the primary worship due only God.

DO ANGELS PUNISH SINNERS?

In the Bible's New Testament, the angel Gabriel suddenly materializes in the great Jewish temple at Jerusalem to tell the old, old priest Zachariah that he'll soon father a child, John The Baptist, the forerunner of Jesus.

But when Zachariah doubts him, Gabriel stikes him dumb.

In the Old Testament, when Egypt's pharoah disregards divine plagues of locusts, frogs and blood and still refuses to allow the Hebrew slaves to leave for the Promised Land, the Angel of Death shows up to kill all firstborn Egyptian sons.

When the orgies at Sodom and Gomorrah got out of hand, three angels showed up to rain down fire and brimstone on the towns -- especially after townsmen tried to rape one of them.

In fact, the Bible is peppered with violent angel acts against wrongdoers -- such as the wholesale massacre of an Assyrian army -- although modern instances of violent angelic wrath are hard to come by. In 14 months of research, I failed to come across one.

Perhaps angels, higher spiritual beings that they are, really act like highly spiritual men we see on earth -- only more so. Gandhi and King used gentle persuasion, not plagues. In the same way, Jesus criticized his chief disciple Peter for heaving a sword to lop off the ear of someone in the crowd that arrested the Nazarene.

"He who lives by the sword will die

by the sword," was Jesus´ comment on Peter´s violent wrath.

HOW SMART ARE ANGELS?

The usual opinion is that the steady rise in living things from virus to vegetable to valedictorian continues right on in the spirit world.

Angels, then, would look on Einstein thinking out his Theory of Relativity as we would a cageful of chimps trying to use a stick to get a banana hanging from the ceiling.

Interestingly, people who allegedly "left" their physical bodies during brushes with death have repeatedly told near-death researchers that they suddenly could think much more clearly and rapidly in their "spirit bodies."

The Middle Ages´ top angel scholar, Thomas Aquinas, said 800 years ago that souls in heaven -- like angels -- "shall survey all... knowledge at the same time by a glance."

Indeed, researcher Raymond Moody was

told by a woman who skirted death that for a moment she knew "all the secrets of the ages, all the meaning of the universe, the stars, the moon, everything."

This flash of universal insight was in images, sounds, thoughts and other forms, but she could not retain them on "returning" to this world.

Green, another researcher, was told by a person whose soul allegedly left his physical body that he was an "eye of gas" able to see and think. And every question he thought of could immediately be answered.

Indeed, artists have often symbolized this superior "heavenly" knowledge -- which apparently includes psychic powers like mind-reading, foreknowledge and so on -- by painting angels´ heads as being covered with eyes.

Maybe Mohammed had "heavenly knowledge" in mind when he said, "Life is a dream; when we die, we wake."

Or as Jesus put it, "Nothing is covered up that will not be revealed..."

Or Paul of Tarsus: "When I was a child, my speech, feelings and thinking were all those of a child. Now that I am a man, I have no more use for childish ways. What we see now is like a dim image in a mirror; (Later) we shall see face to face.

DO ANGELS MARRY?

After Jesus´ triumphal entry into Jerusalem on Palm Sunday a week before his arrest, he was teaching in the Temple area when approached by "Sadducees" -- members of a Jewish sect that did not believe in life after death.

They asked him a hypothetical question about a widow who, in turn, married seven brothers as each of them died. Who was to be her husband in heaven, they asked.".... when the dead rise to life, they will be like the angels in heaven and will not marry," Jesus answered.

Some interpret Jesus´ words as implying that angels are sexless.

Indeed, Christian artists have often blurred sexual distinctions, showing angels as effeminate youths -- although before the 1200s, angels were generally considered masculine.

Kenneth Ring´s recent study of persons brushing with death turned up some near death survivors who reported that supernatural religious beings they encountered spoke with a man´s voice.

But this was not a systematic finding, as Ring did not invariably ask patients about the gender of the religious "Presence" they sometimes encountered.

DO ANGELS TEACH EACH OTHER?

A common view is that stronger angels turn to lesser ones out of love, strengthening their intellects as spiritual beings rise higher and higher toward God, the "sun of spirits."

Lower angels, according to this theory, cannot enlighten higher ones, but just report their state of mind.

The teaching itself supposedly follows our earthly pattern. A complicated truth -- like how insecurity can lead to negative-minded aggressiveness, to use an earthly example -- is broken down into finer points for the student angel to digest little by little till he grasps the whole concept.

WHERE DOES THE WORD "ANGEL" COME FROM?

It´s ancient Greek for "messenger" -- a common job for angels in the Bible.

About 2,700 years ago, Greece´s number one poet, the blind singer Homer, used the word "angels" (angeloi) to refer to ordinary messengers as he wrote about the Trojan War and Oddyseus´ 10-year wanderings from Cyclops to Circe.

In Persian, the related word "angaros" means "courier." And in Sanskrit, the ancient religious language of India, the word-cousin for angel, "angiras," means "divine spirit."

Although the New Testament was written first in Greek, the more ancient Old Testament was composed in Hebrew, where the word for angel is "malakh" (messenger), not "angelos."

WHAT ARE THE SPECIAL FEAST DAYS HONORING DIFFERENT ANGELS?

In 1670, the Catholic Church set aside Oct. 2 as a feast day to honor guardian angels.

In fact, countries like Portugal and cities like Valencia, Spain have had feast days for their national and municipal guardian angels as well.

Meanwhile, Christian festivals on

May 8 and Sept. 29 have acknowledged the warrior angel Michael. And on July 28, Ethiopian and Egyptian Christians have staged the Feast of Uriel, the angel linked to thunderstorms, earthquakes and erupting volcanoes -- but denounced by western European Christians as a false spirit.

In 1590, Pope Sixtus V even okayed a special day for remembering the guardian angel of the Portuguese Empire.

HOW MANY ANGELS ARE THERE?

"Millions of spiritual creatures walk the earth unseen, both when we wake and when we sleep," the blind Puritan poet John Milton put it bluntly.

Trumping Milton, Jewish mystics in the Middle Ages managed to come up with, yes, an exact headcount of 301,655,722. How? They ingeniously changed words to numbers and back again.

Whatever their census, angels are said to outnumber us 4-billion mortals about like the Sioux nation outnumbered

(Illustration 31) An angel at table.

Custer´s Seventh Cavalry.

After all, the more perfect the creatures, the more of them, many churchmen have believed.

Take Jesus´ parable about the shepherd who left behind his 99 sheep to go looking for his one lost sheep.

Ancient Christians liked to compare the one "lost" sheep with the small population of "fallen" humankind. The other 99 faithful sheep stood for the sinless angel world, giving it a 99-to-1 population edge over us -- so the interpretation went.

But Thomas Heywood, an English playwright of the 1600s, warned that zealots counting angels down to the last halo would just "grow from ignorance to error."

And Biblical Job, who lost his family, his livestock and was covered with boils but refused to curse God -- probably had the most practical approach to counting the holy "Breaths of God:"

"Who," he asked, "shall number the armies of the Lord?"

WHAT ARE SOME EXAMPLES OF GUINESS-LIKE RECORDS IN THE WORLD OF ANGEL LEGEND AND LORE?

Here are some nominees:
* Highest: In the Gospel of Peter, two angels bearing Christ´s body up to heaven had heads that nudged against the sky. Meanwhile, an unorthodox Christian group called the Elkesaites spoke of a female angel giant 96 miles high.
* Most specialized: In these days of specialization, few have tasks so narrowly defined as the angel Tzadiquel -- who every Thursday governs the planet Jupiter.
* Most famous angel search: In Milton´s Paradise Lost, after Adam and Eve fall asleep one night in the Garden of Eden, the angel Gabriel, aware that Satan is at large in the area, sends out angel troops to ferret him out. The angel sleuths Ithuriel and Zephon finally turn up Satan squatting toad-like beside Eve´s ear, causing her to have a foul dream. When Ithurial touches Satan with his spear, the metal causes him to resume his true form, so ugly he is unrecognizable.

SOME PEOPLE SAY A GUARDIAN ANGEL MAY
ACTUALLY BE YOUR "HIGHER SELF." WHAT´S
THAT?

For centuries, some mystics have
claimed that your human personality is
just the "tip of the iceberg" of the
"Total You."

The "total you" -- that is, your
"higher self" -- has tremendous mental
power and wisdom in the spirit world.
But just a tiny fraction of that is
available to you in your physical body.

The reason: The earthly soul is
just a split-off "fragment" of this
greater spirit self -- a chip off the
old block, according to this theory.

In fact, this greater "higher self"
supposedly reincarnates on earth over
and over as limited human personalities
to add to its store of wisdom,
knowledge, and ethics.

Indeed, hunches from that "still,
small voice" within us -- it is alleged
-- are sometimes the higher self trying
to communicate with its limited earthly
self.

Just before birth, the soul
allegedly pictures what it hopes to
accomplish on earth in a particular
lifetime.

"One of the regrets of life after
death is the comparison of our original
plan for our life with actual
achievements. It never does come up to
par because when we are in the timeless
and spaceless world, we feel ourselves
to be veritable spiritual giants... We
do not realize..., the restrictions of
time and space," wrote Charles Hampton

in <u>The Transition Called Death.</u>

Was it a guardian angel or just the higher self that suddenly guided the famous naturalist John Muir during a terrifying, life-threatening climb of Mount Ritter?

In a cold sweat over the danger of falling to a glacier below, Muir suddenly "became possessed of a new sense -- my quivering nerves taken over by my other self... became inflexible, my eyes (super-normally) clear, and every rift, flow, niche, and tablet in the cliff ahead was seen through a microscope."

Indeed, some ancient religions held that part of the soul stays separate from the physical body and acts like a personal guardian spirit. The Vikings called their version of this "The Follower" or "The Second One" -- a halfghostly soul-twin who could appear in human form to give advice.

Scientist John Lilly, who in the 1960s tried to set up 2-way communication with dolphins, describes a near-death experience in which he encounters two overwhelmingly loving guardians spirits of his.

"As they move closer and closer, I find less and less of me and more and more of them in my being. They stop at a critical distance and say to me that at this time I have developed only to the point where I can stand their presence at this particular distance. If they came any closer, they would overwhelm me, and I would lose myself as a cognitive entity, merging with them. They further say that I separated them into two because that is my way of perceiving them, but that in reality they are one... They say that I insist on still being an individual, forcing a projection onto them, as if they were two."

Some suggest that the supernaturally loving and knowledgable "beings of light" that near-death patients encounter may merely be their "highest and best selves."

All told, the "higher self" idea may explain some guardian angel happenings. But there's plenty of evidence for plain and ordinary angel guardians, too -- not to mention dead loved ones also getting involved on earth.

CAN ANGELS SUFFER PHYSICAL DISCOMFORT OR BODILY HANDICAPS?

As pure spirits, angels would not be expected to have physical problems.

In fact, persons whose spirits have allegedly left their bodies, often during close calls with death, tell stories that back up this idea.

Mentally ill patients are said at times to become suddenly rational and clear-headed just before death.

On his deathbed, that melancholy -- and deaf -- composer of the early 1800s, Beethoven, announced: "I shall hear!"

"The immediate sensation of many as they get free from the body... is that an instantaneous cure has taken place," writes Charles Hampton in The Transition Called Death.

"One moment there is pain. The next is one of complete relief from pain. The impression is a delightful feeling of lightness and buoyancy" caused by the spirit's suddenly being free of physical gravity.

What's more, near-death patients have told investigators that their spirit bodies -- when outside the physical body -- felt no extremes of temperature.

WHAT HAS BEEN ONE OF THE MOST COMMON ARGUMENTS IN FAVOR OF ANGELS BEING REAL?

For centuries, philosophers have talked about something they call a "chain of being" -- in other words, the stairway of creation upward from atoms to humans to God.

It´s very unlikely, they argue, that human beings are the last step upward on this jampacked staircase before reaching God.

Without a vast world of higher and higher angel ranks, there would be a huge gap in the "chain of being" between humans and God.

As one German philosopher put it, "Nature makes no leaps" either in the visible or the invisible world.

Humans beings, by the way, stand at best halfway up the stairs on the border between flesh and spirit, "a little lower than the angels," in the Bible´s words. But some thinkers suspect we´re far down the lower end.

Our awkward position between creatures that dimly know themselves and superthinking angels was charmingly touched on by British Prime Minister Benjamin Disraeli in 1864: "Is man an ape or an angel? I, my lord, I am on the side of the angels. I repudiate with indignation and abhorrence those newfangled theories (of evolution)."

Or as Blaise Pascal, scientist and mathematician of the 1600s put it, "Man is neither angel nor brute."

Other Books on Angels
and Related Subjects

Adler, Mortimer, The Angels and Us.
Macmillan Publishing Co., New York.
1982.

Asimov, Isaac, Asimov's Guide to the
Bible. Avon Books, New York. 1969.

Bellah, Charles, Celestial Visitors.
Signs Pub. 1938.

Black, David, Ekstasy: Out of the Body
Experiences. Bobbs-Merrill Co.,
Indianapolis. 1975.

Blackmore, Rev. Simon, The Angel World.
John Winterich, Cleveland, Ohio. 1927.

Boros, Ladislaus, Angels and Men.
Seabury Press, New York. 1977.

Boyd, L.M., Boyd's Book of Odd Facts.
New American Library, New York. 1980.

Brewer, Rev. Cobham, A Dictionary of
Miracles. Gale Research Co., Detroit.
1966.

Cameron, Ann, The Angel Book. Ballentine
Books, New York. 1977.

Christopher, Milbourne, Search for the
Soul. Thomas Crowell Publishers, New
York. 1979.

Crookall, Robert, The Supreme Adventure.
James Clarke and Co., London.

Davidson, Gustav, A Dictionary of
Angels. Collier-Macmillan Canada,
Toronto. 1967.

Danielou, Jean, The Angels and Their
Mission. The Newman Press, Westminster,
Maryland.

Delacour, Jean-Baptiste, Glimpses of the
Beyond. Delacorte Press, New York. 1974.

Field, Angels and Ministers of Grace.
Hill and Wang, New York. 1971.

Fodor, Nandor, Encyclopedia of Psychic
Science. The Citadel Press, Secaucus,
N.J.

Fowler, Alfred, Our Angel Friends in
Ministry and Song. (No publisher listed)

Funk and Wagnall's Standard Dictionary
of Folklore.

Gaebelein, Arno, The Angels of God. Our
Hope Publication Office, New York. 1924.

Gilmore, Don, Angels, Angels Everywhere.

Graham, Billy, Angels: God's Secret
Agents. Pocket Books, New York. 1975.

Green, Celia, Out-of-the-Body
Experiences. Hamish Hamilton, London.
1968.

Greenhouse, Herbert, The Astral Journey.

Avon Books, New York. 1976.

Grof, Stanislav, and Halifax, Joan, The Human Encounter with Death. Dutton, N.Y. 1977.

Hahn, Emily, Breath of God. Doubleday and Co., New York. 1971.

Hall, Manley, The Blessed Angels. The Philosophical Research Society, Los Angeles. 1980.

Hampton, Charles, The Transition Called Death. Theosophical Publishing House, Wheaton, Ill. 1943.

Erlendur Haraldsson and Karlis Osis, At the Hour of Death. Avon Books, New York. 1977.

Harrison, Margaret, Angels Then and Now. Branch-Smith, Fort Worth. 1975.

Holzer, Hans, The Ghosts That Walk in Washington. Doubleday and Co., New York. 1971.

Husslein, Joseph, The Spirit World About Us. Bruce Publishing Co., New York. 1934.

Hyslop, James, Psychical Research and the Resurrection. Small, Maynard and Co., Boston. 1908.

Johnson, Raynor, A Religious Outlook for Modern Man. McGraw-Hill, New York. 1963.

Joppie, A.S., The Ministry of Angels.

Baker Book House, Grand Rapids, Mich.
1953.

Latham, Henry, _A Service of Angels_.
Deighton, Bell and Co., Cambridge. 1896.

Leadbeater, C.W., _Invisible Helpers_.
Theosophical Book Concern, Chicago.
1915.

Leadbeater, C.W., _Life After Death_.
Theosophical Publishing House, Madras,
India. 1964.

Leavell, Landrum, _Angels, Angels,
Angels_. Broadman Press, Nashville. 1973.

Lloyd, Marjorie Lewis, _It Must Have Been
an Angel_. Pacific Press Publishing
Association, Mountain View, Calif. 1980.

Lockyer, Herbert, _The Mystery and
Ministry of Angels_. Eerdmans Publishing
Co., Grand Rapids, Mich. 1958.

Lovejoy, Arthur, _The Great Chain of
Being_. Harvard University Press. 1966.

McConkie, Oscar, Jr., _Angels_. Deseret
Book Co., Salt Lake City, Utah. 1975.

Man, Myth and Magic. Cavendish Corp.,
New York. 1970.

Miller, Leslie, _All About Angels_. Regal
Books, Glendale, Calif. 1976.

Milton, John, _Paradise Lost_.

Moody, Raymond, Jr., _Life After Life_.

Mockingbird Books. 1975.

Moody, Raymond, Jr., _Reflections on Life After Life_. Bantam Books, New York. 1978.

Moss, Thelma, _The Probability of the Impossible_. J.P. Tarcher, Los Angeles. 1974.

Mould, Daphne, _Angels of God_. Devin-Adair Co., New York. 1963.

Muldoon, Sylvan, _The Case for Astral Projection_. Aries Press, Chicago. 1936.

Newhouse, Flower, _Natives of Eternity_. J.F. Rowny Press, Santa Barbara, Calif. 1937.

Palmer, Tobias, _An Angel in my House_. Ave Maria Press, Notre Dame, Ind. 1975.

Parente, Pascal, _Beyond Space_. St. Paul Publications, N.Y. 1961.

Paula, Mary, _Presenting the Angels_. Benziger Brothers. 1935.

Peale, Norman Vincent, _The Power of Postive Thinking_. Prentice-Hall, Englewood Cliffs, N.J. 1952.

Rauscher, William, _The Spiritual Frontier_. Doubleday and Co., Garden City, N.Y. 1975.

Regamy, Pie-Raymond, _What is an Angel?_ Hawthorn Books Publishers, N.Y. 1960.

Richards, H.M.S., Jr., Angels -- Secret Agents of God and Satan. Review and Herald Publishing Association, Nashville, Tenn. 1980.

Ring, Kenneth, Life At Death. Coward, McCann and Geoghegan, New York. 1980.

Sabom, Michael, Recollections of Death -- A Medical Investigation. Harper and Row, New York. 1982.

Scheweis, Emil, Angels and Demons According to Lactantius. Catholic Univeristy of America Press, Washington D.C. 1944.

Smith, Susy, Life is Forever. G.P. Putnam's Sons, New York. 1974.

Wallechinsky and Wallace, The People's Almanac 2. Bantam Books, New York. 1978.

Ward, Theodora, Men and Angels. Viking Press, New York. 1969.

Weiss, Jess, The Vestibule. Ashley Books, Port Washington, N.Y. 1972.

Westermann, Claus, God's Angels Need No Wings. Fortress Press. 1979.

Wheeler, David, Journey to the Other Side. Ace Books, New York.

Wilson, Peter, Angels. Pantheon Books, New York. 1980.

The World Almanac Book of the Strange. New American Library, New York.

Index

Colophon

Do You Have a Guardian Angel? was written on an Apple IIe microcomputer using Word Juggler word processing software by Quark. Typesetting was done with a Juki 6100 letter quality computer printer, using a single-strike ribbon. Screening and reduction of photographs was provided by Modernage Publications of Rockledge, Fla. Offset printing and perfect binding was by McNaughton & Gunn of Ann Arbor, Mich. Cover design by Tim Hartsfield. The cover itself is multicolor, with film lamination.

Acknowledgements

Here, in no particular order, are some people and groups that have contributed in important ways to this book, directly or indirectly. Mindful that there will be inevitable omissions, here goes: Jeanne Hoechst-Ronner, Diane Printy and the staff of the Melbourne Public Library, Cathy Schweinsberg and the staff of the Cocoa Public Library, Edna Ronner, Marge Bussey, Marty and Diana Greco and Modernage Publications, Kathy Thorn, Jean and Al Hoechst, Don and Barbara Becker, Dean and Susan Chapman.

Order Form

Mamre Press
315 Riverside Place
Indialantic, Fla. 32903

Please send me _____ copies of the
<u>Do You Have a Guardian Angel</u> at $10.95
each. I understand that I may return
the book for a complete refund if not
totally satisfied.

Name: _____

Address: _____

_____

Zip: _____

Florida residents: Please add 54 cents
sales tax

_____ I don´t want to wait several
weeks for Book Rate. Here is $2.50 for
each book for Air Mail.

Order Form

Mamre Press
315 Riverside Place
Indialantic, Fla. 32903

Please send me _____ copies of the
<u>Do You Have a Guardian Angel</u> at $10.95
each. I understand that I may return
the book for a complete refund if not
totally satisfied.

Name: _____

Address: _____

_____

Zip: _____

Florida residents: Please add 5 4 cents
sales tax

_____ I don´t want to wait several
weeks for Book Rate. Here is $2.50 for
each book for Air Mail.